RUSSIAN MEDIAEVAL ARCHITECTURE

Church of the Intercession on the River Nerl, at Bogolyubovo, near Vladimir. 1166

RUSSIAN MEDIAEVAL ARCHITECTURE.

WITH AN ACCOUNT OF THE TRANSCAUCASIAN STYLES AND THEIR INFLUENCE IN THE WEST

BY

DAVID RODEN BUXTON

HACKER ART BOOKS
NEW YORK, N.Y. 1975

First published 1934, Cambridge
Reissued 1974 by Hacker Art Books, Inc.
Library of Congress Catalogue Card Number 73-81682
ISBN 0-87817-005-7
Printed in the United States of America

CONTENTS

CONTENTS

ILLUSTRATIONS

TEXT-FIGURES

SUMMARY OF PLATES

ILLUSTRATIONS

NOTE ON ILLUSTRATIONS

I have to thank Professor E. H. Minns for two interiors [Plates 48–9]; for two views of Moscow [Plates 50, 2; 51, 1]; and for the books from which certain Ukrainian views [Plates 56, 2, 3; 57] were reproduced. (Those on Plate 57 with the sanction of the Orchis Verlag, Munich.)

The Rev. H. W. Harcourt kindly lent ten valuable photographs of Armenian buildings taken by himself in 1921–2 [Plates 83, 1; 88, 1; 89; 90].

The block for an interior [Plate 47] was supplied by the Oxford University Press.

Professor Josef Strzygowski of Vienna kindly allowed the reproduction of the six plans on page 83 from his work *Die Baukunst der Armenier und Europa*.

The following drawings and photographs derive from various Russian sources: Plates 7, 4; 18–20; 28, 2; 56, 1, 4; 72, 2; 73, 1, 2; 74, 2. All the plans' and sections (except those of Transcaucasia) are also taken from Russian books. I have, however, myself added the domes in D, p. 65.

The remaining 192 photographs reproduced are from my own negatives. The following date from 1927: Plates 50, 1; 51, 2; 55, 4; 64, 1, 2; 65, 2. Among the rest, all those of the central Russian and Volga towns, and most of Moscow, as well as those of Novgorod, Pskov and Kiev, were taken in 1928. All those of wooden architecture and of Transcaucasia, as well as the one of Veliki Ustyug and some of Moscow are the product of my last Russian journey, in 1932.

PREFACE

This book is the outcome of an interest in Russian architecture originally stimulated in 1927, when I visited the Soviet Union for the first time. The bulk of the photographs were accumulated in the course of two long journeys undertaken for that special purpose in the summer and autumn of 1928 and 1932. Between these dates, owing to preoccupation at Cambridge in a wholly different field of learning, I was obliged to leave the subject until an opportunity should come to pursue it. Since the middle of last year, however, I have been able freely to devote myself to the absorbing study which now finds fruit in this volume.

I have no doubt that many students of mediaeval architecture will welcome an account, short and imperfect though it be, of a style so much neglected, and on which literature is so scarce, that there are few to recognise its existence as a possible subject of study. At the same time I hope that even those who take no special interest in architecture may enjoy the illustrations, which in this country have at least the merit of novelty.

To the writer, however, these pictures must always have a meaning which others cannot share with him. Journeys in obscure parts of Russia could only be performed under conditions so peculiar and so uniformly difficult that to fulfil any part of one's programme seemed at the time a notable achievement. One and all the photographs recall, sometimes with startling vividness, incidents and experiences of travel, with their attendant thoughts and emotions. There are those which suggest moments of high satisfaction—the end of a tedious and sleepless railway journey lasting through the night; the first sight of some remote village, the goal of a long day's tramp through the forests round the White Sea; the triumphant conclusion of a stiff climb in the Caucasus.

PREFACE

There are others whose message is painful, so that one prefers to turn the page lest the memories they harbour should come back too forcibly.

My photographs, moreover, have lived through dangerous vicissitudes, and their survival calls for thankfulness. Those of 1928 underwent abuse and violation truly horrifying to a photographer; a few were destroyed or lost, but the remainder I carried home in safety. Those, on the other hand, of 1932, were seized and retained by the Customs authority of Batum, and for months their recovery remained a matter of uncertainty.

In the hope of increasing the value of the book to those more deeply interested, I have included a number of plans and sections, especially in Part I, as materials on Russia are so difficult of access. I have refrained, however, from fully describing these diagrams in the text; they are left to convey their own message to those who care to study them. The two maps, I believe, will be acceptable to all. In them prominence is given more especially to places of architectural importance, and many small villages are included solely because they find mention in the text. Modern towns are mostly omitted, but frontiers, for the sake of convenience, are shown following the often fantastic courses which recent political changes have given them.

It is not merely from a sense of duty that I here make known my indebtedness to those who have helped in the creation of this book. Firstly I would offer my cordial thanks to Professor Minns of Cambridge, who has given freely, and on many matters, help and advice which he alone is able to give; and has shown an appreciation and tolerance which, in view of his immense learning, have been a particular pleasure . and encouragement to me. To the staff of the University Press I would express my gratitude for the trouble they have taken in the production of the book. My obligations in the matter of illustrations are particularised in a special note, and the great deal I owe to the authors of works in various languages may be gathered from the bibliography.

But my greatest debt remains to be recorded. To Charles Roden and Dorothy Frances Buxton is due the very existence of this book, and all of mine that it contains. For assuredly, without their constant help, not only in practical, but also in more abstract ways, there would have been no journeys in Eastern Europe; no photographs; no book. To them, therefore, I dedicate it; and I am glad at this moment, when about to sail for another quarter of the globe, to leave in their hands a small token of true appreciation.

D. R. B.

LONDON
October 1933

NOTE ON TRANSLITERATION

A standard system has been used in the transliteration of Russian words and place names. The following list contains only the less obvious English equivalents employed.

Russian e	English e (generally pronounced ye)
ё (printed e)	yo
й (following vowels other than и and ы)	y
ы	y
iй (revised spelling ий)	i
ый	y
ь and ъ	(omitted)
ж	zh (as *s* in *leisure*; French j)
х	kh (as *ch* in *loch*; German ch)

The other consonants used have their ordinary English values. The vowels all denote single sounds, as in most continental languages, not as in English.

The word собор (originally denoting *assembly* or *synod*) is applied by extension of the meaning to important churches in Russia. Although this word is generally translated 'cathedral', a Bishop's seat is not implied, and I have sometimes used the simple transliteration *sobor* instead.

Where a transliterated Russian word appears for the first time, it is always given in the nominative singular.

PREFACE TO THE 1975 EDITION

When I roamed the Soviet Union as a youth more than forty years ago I was one of a mere handful of foreign travellers, compared with the many thousands who now go there every year. Probably for that reason, among others, the arts of Russia—even the icons—had few devotees among the general public in western Europe. So this early work, though my pride and joy at the time, and though reviewed very appreciatively by several connoisseurs, enjoyed but a small circulation and was never reprinted.

As a full revision of the book is not possible I shall simply comment as follows on some of the plates:—

(a) Although many old buildings have been destroyed in the last few decades, others have been restored with taste and skill. This is true, for instance, of that great architectural complex, the "Trinity monastery of St. Sergius" at Sergievo (now Zagorsk). The churches of the Trinity (plate 17,2) and of the Holy Ghost (plate 21,4) have had their unsightly plain roofs removed and the beautiful lines of their "superposed" vaults and arches revealed—as the architects of Pskov who originally built them would no doubt have wished.

(b) Unhappily, buildings of the "Moscow Baroque" have fared badly compared with those of more purely Russian character, and I am informed that neither of the churches shown in plate 58 survives. I must also correct an error in the original captions to this section: the two upper figures in plate 60 represent tower-churches on the walls of the Don Monastery, not the Novodevichi Monastery.

(c) In the field of wooden architecture constant losses are inevitable, and they can be tragic. An example is the loss of the great "tented" church at Belaya Sluda (plates 68-9), one of the finest examples of that ancient architectural form, which was struck by lightning and burnt down in 1962, having stood for 320 years. On the credit side, the remarkable 18th-century churches at Kem (plate 72) and Kizhi (plates 75-7) have been stripped of their ugly external boarding so that the original horizontal timbers are now properly exposed to view.

Nowadays, those with a taste for wooden churches and peasant architecture in general can partially satisfy their curiosity without undertaking any extensive travels, since examples of such buildings have been brought in and re-erected in several village museums or "skansens". A notable one has been established at Kizhi among the waters of Lake Onega—a place already referred to above and described in the text of this book. It now has a fascinating museum of wooden architecture and is being developed as a tourist resort. Kolomenskoe near Moscow is the scene of a similar enterprise, specializing in timber-built fortifications. Some wooden churches have also been re-erected at Suzdal, at Kostroma on the Volga, near Novgorod, and in several Ukrainian cities. In the Baltic republics there is a village museum at Riga (Latvia), while another is in course of formation outside Tallinn (Esthonia). There is, therefore, some comfort even for those who would prefer to see all these rustic buildings in their native countryside.

This book still seems to me an adequate introduction to a subject still greatly neglected: Russian architecture has since been treated (as far as English-language publications are concerned) only as part of the broader subject of the Russian arts.° Now that an interest in all things Russian is so widespread I feel that this reprint is amply justified, and may serve the book's intended purposes better than the original edition. Cambridge, 1973

° See especially G.H. Hamilton, *The Art and Architecture of Russia* (Pelican History of Art), London, 1954.

PART I: RUSSIA

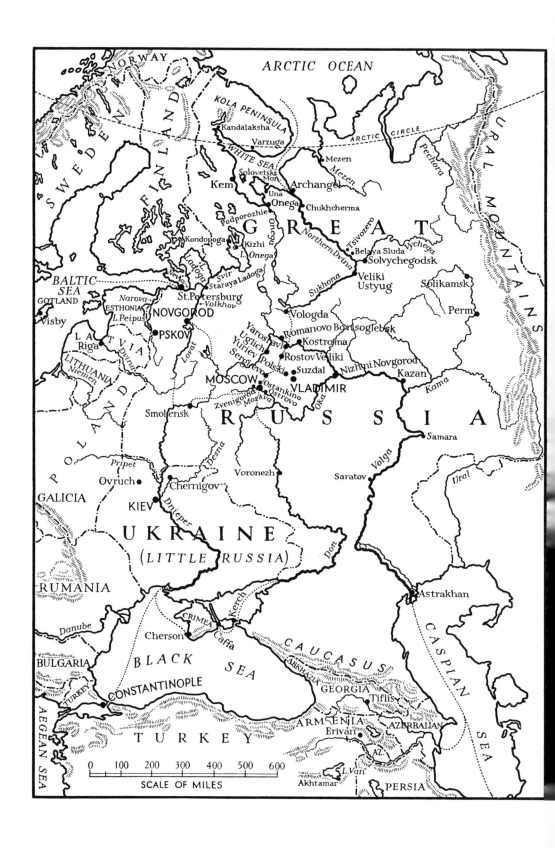

INTRODUCTORY

THE architecture of Russia has not been allowed the place it deserves in the history of the architectures of the world. In general histories such as those of Fergusson and Rosengarten, it is described as a debased Byzantine, owing something to the Tartars, but nothing more than its very degeneration to the Russians themselves.

The first to make known the Russian style to the Western public was Viollet le Duc who, in a volume published in 1877, set forth his conclusions as to the derivation of Russian architectural forms from eastern sources. Viollet le Duc's attitude was tolerant, even appreciative; but his conclusions were entirely mistaken. Never having set foot in Russia, he could work only on second-hand materials sent from Moscow; moreover, it is said that his approach was not free from Slavophilic bias, which led him to exaggerate the Asiatic at the expense of the European connections in Russian art. Viollet le Duc's work, therefore, has little value at the present time, and since this, together with Fergusson's inaccurate and recklessly critical account, were the only materials available, until recently, bearing on the Russian style, it is not surprising that the architectural world has remained either uninformed or grossly misinformed on the subject.

Even in Russia itself the national style of architecture provoked no serious study until the end of the last and the beginning of the present century, and no literature sufficiently palatable to appeal to the public appeared until Grabar's great work began to be published in 1909. Intensive study of all aspects of the national life and culture in Russia was an outcome of the Slavophil movement. This study brought in its train a crop of literature on the arts, and active publication was in full swing when the War and Revolution intervened. A number of works, then actually in course of publication, were interrupted, and their concluding volumes never saw the light. Now, fortunately, there is some prospect of publication being resumed. Since the revolution a few books have appeared in French and in German, but the English language remains without literature on the subject of Russian Architecture.[1]

Few students of architecture, possessed of material from which to judge, could now deny the interest and value of this much neglected study. But it can still be argued that the Russian style is one of the world's lesser expressions of artistic genius. Loukomski, indeed, speaks of it in these words:

(The study of Grabar's volumes) nous revèle que la Russie renfermait tout un monde de rêves artistiques qu'elle savait réaliser avec un élan et un génie qui la placent, sinon au même rang que la France et l'Italie, du moins à côté de l'Angleterre, l'Espagne, et l'Allemagne.

There cannot be many, however, who will admit such a comparison between our own great cathedrals and even the finest creations of Russian genius. One must acknowledge that such heights of architectural achievement were never reached in Russia.

It is not difficult to find reasons for this deficiency. There prevail in Russia general and almost inevitable geographical conditions inimical to the development of a great art: diffuseness of the population; paucity of urban centres; their immense distance apart and the difficulty of communications. Moreover, historical and religious causes conspired to isolate Russia from the general stream of cultural evolution which affected the whole of western Europe. The adoption by Russia of the Greek, rather than the Latin Church, meant the creation of a permanent barrier between herself and her western neighbours. These causes together contributed to the retardation of Russian civilisation centuries behind that of western Europe.

Russia's own internal history was, however, the most potent of

---

[1] There are two chapters in *The Russian Arts* by Rosa Newmarch (Herbert Jenkins, 1916) and a short account in the fourteenth (but not in any previous) edition of the *Encyclopaedia Britannica*.

disturbing influences, both in the general progress of her civilisation, and in the development of a national style of architecture. Each architectural centre was in turn destroyed and abandoned, and the art grew up anew in some other province; the greatest of these breaks, that of the Mongol invasion in the thirteenth century, resulted practically in loss of the building art, and the new style of Moscow grew up slowly and laboriously with the help of architects from abroad, and from north-west Russia, which had escaped the disastrous onslaughts of the Mongols.

Later on, it was the Russian Church itself which hindered the free and natural development of the arts. The Church, essentially and above all things conservative, saw with hostile eyes the new architectural features—derived from the old wooden architecture of north Russia—which began to usurp the place of traditional Byzantine forms about the beginning of the sixteenth century. In the middle of the seventeenth, just when the national style was showing its greatest originality and fertility, Nikon, the Russian Patriarch, forbade the use of conical towers, and other attractive innovations of the time, as contrary to Church tradition, and attempted to standardise the "sacred five-domed church" on a square plan. Only in far northern Russia, where the builders of wooden churches felt relatively secure from the Patriarch's censure, was the development of architecture left for a time unhampered. This ecclesiastical edict of 1650 is largely responsible for the monotonous omnipresence of the five-domed church, a uniformity one is apt wrongly to attribute to lack of initiative on the part of the Russian builders.

The final blow to Russian architecture came at the beginning of the eighteenth century, when Peter the Great prohibited all building in stone anywhere but in St Petersburg. Petersburg he built on the model of a west European city, introducing mostly inferior architects from the western countries to work there. Since the foundation of St Petersburg, a sort of neo-classical architecture, the so-called "Empire" style, was used in Russia. It was followed in the middle of the last century by a revival of the national architecture brought to light by the Slavophils, and a number of unsatisfactory creations in a "pseudo-Russian" style appeared in Moscow and elsewhere.

Since the Revolution a new style again has become rooted in Russia, as widely different from the neo-classical as was that style from the traditional Russian. It shows the same general tendencies as the modern architecture of Germany and other European countries, and of America; whether anything distinctively Russian will develop from it, remains to be seen.

It appears, then, that architecture in Russia has had a somewhat discontinuous and cataclysmic history. That steady, uninterrupted development which can be traced in most of the western countries has no counterpart in Russia. One does not find, as in the West, an abundance of monuments of all periods spread widely over the country. On the contrary, in restricted areas and for brief periods one sees outbursts of building activity, to be succeeded by long periods of decay. Always, however, the art was resuscitated somewhere, and an orderly process of evolution can be and has been traced, linking up the isolated fragments of Russian architectural history into a connected whole.

From the earliest centre of culture in what is now Russia, the principality of Kiev on the River Dnieper, the style, differing little at that stage from the typical Byzantine of Constantinople, spread to two new centres where it survived the downfall of the mother country. These were Novgorod in north-west Russia, and Vladimir, on an affluent of the Volga to the east of Moscow. In the first of these areas architecture ran a long course of evolution, but at Vladimir it survived scarcely a hundred years, for the Mongol incursion of 1238 put a final stop to building activity all over that part of the country.

With the emancipation of Russia from the Tartars in the fourteenth and fifteenth centuries a new period of building began, centred in the rising city of Moscow. This period was to see the development of a truly national and original style, compounded of various elements, but rooted essentially in two traditions: the Byzantine tradition of Constantinople, much modified though it was in the architecture of Vladimir, and the wooden tradition of north Russia, which gave the Moscow style its most distinctive character. Not until the sixteenth, and, more especially, the seventeenth century, did any style find a really wide distribution in Russia. But at that time the style of Moscow spread far and wide over the whole country, and it remains an essential and inseparable part of the Russian landscape.

From a consideration of the many consecutive styles that have flourished in Russia, there emerge some general characters common to them all. The buildings are small. Excepting some of the earliest churches of Kiev and Novgorod, which were built by Greeks, and a few of the latest, dating from the seventeenth century, most Russian churches seem by our exalted standards mere chapels, however often dignified with the name of "cathedral".[1]

There are churches in Moscow and Yaroslavl which may be described as large, or even enormous. But they are so only by local standards. It is certainly true that the tendency in Russia was always to build many small churches, rather than to concentrate all the efforts of the community on a single great church, as was the frequent practice in western Europe. This does not mean that the conscious intention of the Russians was to sacrifice quality to quantity. The fact is explained by the widespread custom in ancient Russia of building churches privately—large or small, elaborate or severely simple, according to the means of the builders. There was much individualist competition in church building. Every guild of traders or artisans, every individual citizen of wealth and position, would build a private church in a spirit of rivalry. Thus has a large proportion of the innumerable churches in Russia come into existence.

Many small towns, especially those of the north, which have long lost the importance they once enjoyed as trading places, contain a quantity of churches out of all proportion to their population. Most of them are

[1] See Note on Transliteration at the beginning of this book.

due to the initiative of individual traders; some are large and imposing, the majority small and insignificant. There seems sometimes to have been a sad want of resource, and one may find two churches of identical design standing side by side. Often in such cases the beauty of a place lies not in the individual buildings, but in the *ensemble* as seen from a distance. The many towers and cupolas disposed in clusters or scattered singly along the horizon, give to such little towns as attractive a sky-line as can well be imagined.

Wonderfully picturesque groupings are common in Russia, especially where religious and secular buildings are closely associated, as in a fortified monastery, or a well-filled Kremlin. There are many Kremlins (fortresses) in Russia, but the Kremlin of Moscow, with its three cathedrals, its picturesque wall with towers of all shapes, and the great belfry of Ivan Veliki dominating the whole, is no doubt the finest of them all [see Plates 64, 65].

Monasteries are scattered throughout the country, and many are strongly fortified, like those which fringe the southern outskirts of Moscow, and which in mediaeval times served to protect the capital from the ever present danger of attack from the south. Other famous fortified monasteries are those of the north—Solovetski on an island in the White Sea, Belozerski and Prilutski in the Government of Vologda —and many others.

One feature of their religious architecture the Russians inherited from the Byzantines and preserved almost unchanged until their national style expired at the end of the seventeenth century. This is the simple quadrangular plan, in which four central piers arranged in a square support the principal cupola. It was probably derived from a cruciform plan in which the corners had been filled in to give support to the walls of the four arms; mechanically the type is a very perfect one, for all thrusts[1] are efficiently counteracted. The four extra domes, when present, are arranged on the corners, not on the arms of the cross.

[1] The outward pressure exerted by a dome or other vault, as distinct from the vertical pressure, or load.

This plan follows a type which appeared first in Constantinople in the Nea or "New Church" built by the Emperor Basil I;[1] thence it was no doubt introduced into Russia, where it became quite universal, so much so that any departure from it was apt to be frowned upon by the Church.

The Russians indeed were not original in this matter. They quickly rejected the more complex plan seen in the cathedrals of St Sophia at Kiev and Novgorod. Having made this simpler form their own, they never altered it in any essential particular. (See pp. 22 and 31 for the simpler plans at Novgorod and Vladimir.) The only considerable exceptions to the rule are the wooden churches of the north and in the Ukraine, together with those in brick which take after them most directly, and are therefore almost independent of the Byzantine tradition.

Outwardly the Russian churches are always tall, tending to be much taller in proportion than those of the Byzantine style proper. Bell towers also abound, and in this the Russian style differs markedly from the Byzantine of Constantinople and the Balkans. It has been said that dwellers in flat countries always tend to build high, a theory certainly substantiated on the endless plains of central Russia.

Architectural effect was aimed at only outside. The interiors of these churches form no part of the general conception, and do not vary greatly. They are always dark, a feeble light entering by slit-like windows. They are always short but lofty, and the eye is led upwards to the central cupola; there are no long vistas as in western churches.

Since the fifteenth century a characteristically Russian structure, the *iconostas*, was used in all churches. This is a screen completely separating the body of the church from the sanctuary (*bema*). It is penetrated by three doors, the central one being the "Royal" or "Holy" door, through which only priests may enter. Originally there was nothing more than a low barrier or balustrade dividing off the sanctuary. This came to be used as a stand for icons (whence the name *iconostas*); icons were added in successive rows, one above the other, until a high screen

[1] See pp. 84 and 100.

resulted. In the richer churches it was sumptuously ornamented in silver and gilt [Plates 47–9].

In decoration one may observe the common eastern tendency to diffusion over wide surfaces, rather than concentration on particular elements in the structure, to which it is desired to give prominence. Characteristic, too, is the lavish use of colour, whether on the outside walls or within, where every available space is often covered with fresco. Whether the Russians took the path of least resistance, adopting the simpler forms of surface decoration in preference to carving in hard materials, is doubtful. Their choice was governed largely by the material they had to deal with, and by certain features of their churches inherited from Byzantium, and preserved by conditions in Russia. Their material was brick, and this they covered with plaster or stucco. Stone was seldom available, and, except at Vladimir, practically never used. The Byzantine tradition provided churches with small windows and large wall space, and this feature naturally remained, in fact was intensified, in a country of cold winters and hot summers. Mosaics were abandoned in favour of frescoes, and this, again, was probably the simple result of the scarcity in Russia of materials appropriate for mosaics.

I must refer finally to that most conspicuous feature, which first and last strikes the foreigner as characteristic of and essential to the Russian churches—the bulbous dome. In spite of theories, both old and new, which affirm the contrary, there can be no reasonable doubt that this is a truly native creation, adopted first in the brick buildings of Novgorod about the twelfth century; the account of Novgorod will give an opportunity for the elaboration of this subject. The "onion" dome is, in any case, the most universally popular of architectural forms in Russia, and there can be scarcely a church in the country, stone, brick, or wooden, without it.

In a Russian church the worshippers stand, or else they kneel, to prostrate themselves repeatedly with foreheads to the ground. Before their eyes the complex ceremonial of the Eastern Church proceeds. The long-haired priest and deacons in their gorgeous robes emerge and retreat through the Holy Door, or move among the congregation to swing a censer before every sacred shrine and picture. Clouds of incense hang in the air, rendering yet more mysterious the dim recesses of the church.

Perhaps one should say that these things were so, for even now they are ceasing to be, and before long will be of the past alone. The Church drags on with difficulty in these times; even the old drop away, while a new religion and a new ideal are set before the young. But we are thinking here of the Church as it was, with power unchallenged from outside, and holding the people, for good or ill, in unquestioning submission. Undoubtedly the Church did minister to the spiritual and emotional needs of the populace; their life would have been poorer without it, poor though was that life at best.

The sombre lighting, allowing little to the gaze of the congregation but the gorgeous *iconostas*, dimly lit by candles, helped to create a strange atmosphere of unreality in these Russian churches. The sonorous chanting of the priests; the marvellous sound of the choir, singing unaccompanied; the scent of incense in the air—all this added much to a scene whose almost theatrical splendour was alone enough to draw a congregation too used to the commonplacenesses of life. The church was a place of escape from surroundings often colourless and sordid.

It cannot be said that the Russians as a race were successful builders. They repeatedly relied upon foreigners. Nor have they ever become real masters of building technique. The surviving specimens of their art may very commonly be seen slanting dangerously from the perpendicular, and to this day the Russian builders seem unwilling to waste their time in the laying of solid foundations. A certain slovenliness, a want of thoroughness, a love of display rather than of sound construction, seem ever to have been the weaknesses of Russian craftsmen. The facts of history and geography provide a ready and sufficient explanation.

The Russian style embodies much that fails to appeal to western taste. Evidently it has never made much impression on foreign peoples, for no other style in the world has been influenced by it. It has absorbed much, but has given nothing. One must admit that this style does not live up to many abstract principles of "good art" and "good taste". It certainly conforms to few or none of Fergusson's "true principles of beauty in art" heavily elaborated in his *History of Architecture*. Perhaps the undoubted fact that the Russian style did appeal to the taste of vast populations, and even now at times calls forth the admiration of a Westerner, is proof enough that Fergusson's principles are fallible, his intolerance and contempt uncalled for. One prefers Viollet le Duc's attitude, thus expressed in the concluding paragraph of his pioneer book on Russian architecture:

It is not necessary that every race, in order to take part in the common effort of human progress, should possess the same feeling on every point, the same means of expression. Variety is no obstacle to harmony, it is in fact one of its essential conditions; and complete understanding between all nations—if ever established—will come from free expression of the tastes and tendencies of each one.

Stone carving from St Dmitri, Vladimir, representing
the Ascension of Alexander the Great

HISTORICAL OUTLINE

1. KIEV

Long before anything like a Russian civilisation came into being, there existed colonies of Greeks on the Black Sea coast of what is now Russia, especially in the Crimea, where such cities as Cherson and Theodosia have been the scenes of fruitful excavation in recent times. The Greek settlements formed but a fringe along the southern edge of the vast steppe stretching without known limit to the north and east. This was the country of the nomadic Scythians, who, judging by the works of art unearthed from their burial places—the "kurgans" of southern Russia—had attained to some degree of civilisation.

At that time, however, the territory now called Russia was not inhabited by people of Slavonic race. In the south were Greeks and Scythians; in the north various Finnish tribes which the Slavs, in the course of their history, have steadily displaced, and partly absorbed. It is thought that the centre of dispersal of the Slavs was that part of the Carpathian region now known as Galicia. From about the sixth century onwards they spread in all directions from this centre: southwards into the Balkans, westwards through Germany as far as the Elbe, northwards and eastwards into Poland and Russia.

These Eastern Slavs were now in possession of an essential trade route between the Black Sea and the Baltic. Several towns, afterwards to acquire great importance, grew up on or near its course. Such were Kiev, Smolensk and Novgorod. It was a water route, as have been all the major trade routes in Russia. Sea-going vessels could penetrate from the Gulf of Finland, through the Neva and Lake Ladoga, up the River Volkhov to Novgorod. Thence smaller boats could proceed upstream to a point connected by a portage with the upper course of the

Dnieper. Only one further obstruction stood in the way of a clear passage to the Black Sea. This was a dangerous stretch of rapids on the lower Dnieper, at the head of which lies Kiev, where the cargoes were taken on shore.

These towns were loosely federated, and lacked any sort of central administration. They were in nominal subjection to the Khazars, a Turkish people whose Khan claimed tribute from the Russians. Realising their own incoherence, and the danger of annihilation by nomad tribes always on the move in the steppes to the east, such leaders as the Russians had, decided to invite a foreign people to govern them. In the year 862 they appealed to the "Varyags", a people apparently of Scandinavian race, to send rulers, and they were not slow in complying with this request. A certain Rurik established himself as Prince of Kiev, and from this as capital he organised the first Russian state.

The Slavs at this time were Pagans, and there is every reason to suppose that they built wooden temples. But neither of these, nor of any other form of pagan architecture, does any trace remain. The history of architecture, as of art generally in Russia, dates from the official adoption of Christianity in the tenth century. In Russia, more perhaps than in any other country, art and religion were inseparably associated until modern times.

In 988 Vladimir, Prince of Kiev, decided to introduce Christianity as his state religion. The choice of that form of worship practised in Constantinople was natural, for relations with the eastern metropolis had long been frequent and intimate, and Russian traders were well known there. There were already Christian communities in Russia, notably at Cherson, in the Crimea, and from here Vladimir imported Greek priests to Kiev. He was no half-hearted convert. He ordered his people to be driven down into the River Dnieper and there forcibly baptised.

The conversion of Russia to the Greek Orthodox faith brought tremendous consequences in its train. It was the most powerful factor making for the isolation of Russia from western Europe throughout the

Middle Ages, especially since 1054, the date of the final schism between the Churches of Greece and Rome. And it determined the whole course of development of Russia's art and architecture.

With the Orthodox Church came the architecture characteristic of it then, as it still is now—the Byzantine style. This style was then undergoing its period of greatest expansion—the neo-Byzantine period, characterised by the raising of domes on drums[1] which greatly add to their external effect. The earliest churches of Kiev were most probably built by Greek architects from Cherson, and were purely Byzantine. The earliest and simplest type of plan at Kiev, afterwards universally adopted in Russia, was the plain square with four central pillars supporting a cupola[2] through the intervention of pendentives.[3] Three apses[4] corresponding to the tripartite arrangement of the interior projected at the eastern end.

The plan of St Sophia (B, p. 14) is more complex. Only the central portion of the present plan is original, and even this has been considerably altered; the recent researches of Morgilevski and Brunov have, however, made possible a restoration (C, p. 14). There are five aisles in the original church, but an open gallery seems to have encircled it outside. Inside, the outer pair of side aisles has an upper storey or gallery (section, A, p. 14), and this was formerly carried round the west end of the building, at the same distance from the centre, supported across the nave by a pair of columns similar to those in the transepts. Thus the middle of the church presented the form of a cross with three

[1] The drum is a cylindrical structure raising the springing of the dome to a height above its original position. The drum rests, as the dome proper originally did, directly on the four central arches of the church and the pendentives included between them.

[2] The word cupola, though really meaning the same as dome, is here used to include both the dome and its drum.

[3] Each pendentive fills up the corner between two adjacent arches. It rises in the form of a spherical triangle; its lower corner coincides with the springing of the arches, while its two upper corners meet those of their fellows at the crowns of the arches. The four together thus provide a circular base for the dome or its drum.

[4] A semicircular or polygonal termination at the eastern end of a church.

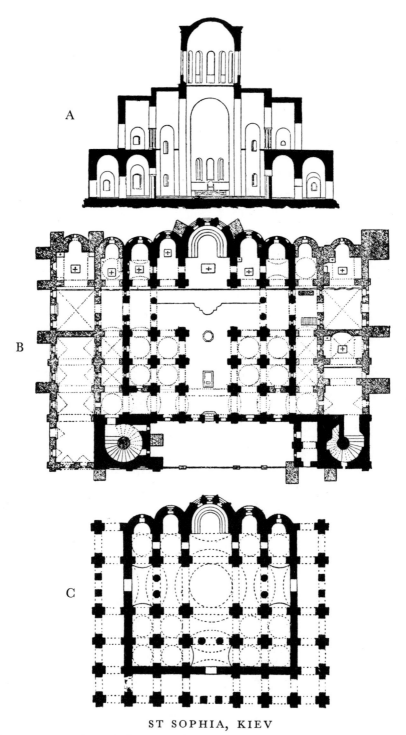

ST SOPHIA, KIEV

A. Transverse section of the part of the building shown in C. Note the upper
galleries of the side aisles. B. Plan of the church as it is now. The parts shown in black
are generally thought to be original. C. Restoration by Brunov. Same scale as B.

similar arms; only the eastern arm was different. This spacious central cross, well lit by the windows in the drum of the central cupola, was sharply marked off from the dimly illumined aisles and galleries surrounding it.

For some time it has been known that a close resemblance exists between the plan of St Sophia and that of a church at Mokvi in Abkhazia (Georgia). Strzygowski and others have deduced a Caucasian influence at Kiev, and have assumed that Armenian or Georgian architects were employed there. The plan of Mokvi, however, is almost unique in Transcaucasia, and there is no evidence to show that such a type was ever widespread there. Moreover, as Brunov points out, the churches of Mokvi and Kiev are in other respects so different that the connection cannot be other than remote and indirect. He is convinced that the plan in question was developed at Constantinople, where he has found it in church foundations of early date. Thence it spread to the Caucasian region and to Russia, as well as eastwards as far as Mesopotamia.

St Sophia at Kiev was founded by Vladimir's successor, Yaroslav the Great, in 1037, to celebrate his victory over the nomad Pechenegs. It is one of very few churches of this period to have retained any approach to its original form. But this applies only to the interior; outside, except for the five original apses, its initial form is completely obscured by seventeenth-century additions in the highly displeasing style known as "Ukrainian Baroque" [Plates 1 and 57]. The original cupola (there was probably only one) consisted of a plain drum with saucer-shaped or hemispherical dome. Now, there are a number of accessory cupolas with much contorted golden domes in the baroque fashion. The same applies to the other Byzantine churches of Kiev; only in Chernigov can a nearer approach be seen to a Byzantine exterior. At the small town of Ovruch is a church perhaps giving the best idea of the architecture of this period, but it is the result of a complete restoration in 1908.

Kiev in the time of Vladimir and Yaroslav was a splendid city which excited the admiration of every traveller. She held intercourse with the western countries, and her Princes, accepted on equal terms by all fellow-sovereigns, often married their daughters into the royal houses of western Europe. But the splendour of Kiev was short-lived. Towards the end of the eleventh century internal disputes were weakening the country. At the same time a drift of population eastwards was altering the centre of Slav settlement from the Kiev-Novgorod axis towards the Volga, and the Princes of Kiev began to set their eyes on distant colonies. In 1109 Andrey Bogolyubski actually deserted the mother town and made his capital in one of the new colonies of the Volga basin —the village, as it then was, of Vladimir. Fearing possible rivalry, he marched on Kiev and sacked it. The old capital was now rapidly decaying, and little was left to the destructive hand of the Mongol invaders when they reached the town a hundred and thirty years later.

The story of architecture in Russia must be taken up again in two new areas: at Vladimir, the new capital of the Rurik dynasty, and at Novgorod, which for centuries after the fall of Kiev remained a prosperous and independent city. Since building was active in the latter place from almost as early a date as in Kiev, and since the architecture of these two cities shows a particularly close relationship, the turn of Novgorod comes first.

2. NOVGOROD AND PSKOV

Novgorod was already, in the tenth century, the most important town in the northerly part of the great trade route between the Baltic and the Black Sea, "from the land of the Varyags to the land of the Greeks". This route was then the central axis of Slav population in eastern Europe. Although originally part of the principality of Kiev, Novgorod increasingly asserted her independence, and developed a democratic constitution of her own, in contrast to the autocratic régimes of Kiev and Vladimir. From the death of Vladimir Monomakh in 1125, Novgorod ceased to recognise the sovereignty of Kiev.

Placed in a swampy country where nature provided but scant means of subsistence, Novgorod was essentially a commercial city—owed, in fact, her existence to commerce. Water communications brought her in touch with all parts of Russia and with the west of Europe. The principal thoroughfare was the Volkhov-Lovat-Dnieper route to Kiev, and on to Constantinople, with which city, even after the Mongol invasion of southern Russia, Novgorod held intercourse. This line was closely linked with the Volga route to the Caspian Sea, while the (Western) Dvina gave an outlet to the Baltic at Riga, as an alternative to the route via Lake Ladoga, the Neva, and the Gulf of Finland (see map).

Enterprising traders of the Hanseatic League early established themselves in the eastern Baltic. They founded Riga in 1160. They penetrated the Neva and the inland lakes of northern Russia to establish connections with Novgorod, whose traders remained always middlemen, not themselves attempting navigation on the open sea. In the eleventh and twelfth centuries trade was particularly active with Lübeck, the capital of the Hanseatic League, and with Visby on the island of Gotland, whose architecture shows conspicuous traces of a Byzantine influence.

Novgorod was a great colonising state, and simultaneously with the occupation of the Volga basin by Kiev, Novgorod was spreading her colonists all over northern Russia, from the Baltic to the White Sea and eastwards even beyond the Urals. As the result of active colonisation from these two original sources—Kiev and Novgorod—the centre of Russian population moved eastwards. The same tendency to eastward penetration found expression in the sixteenth and seventeenth centuries in the colonisation of Siberia, and at a later time in the conquest of central Asia, and other ambitions of Russian imperialism.

The expansion of Novgorod in the vast area of northern Russia was by no means entirely peaceable. Along with her traders, penetrating the northern watercourses, came river pirates (*ushkúynik*) living at the expense of the native population. The Finnish tribes, however, from whom the Novgorodians exacted tribute in the form of furs and foodstuffs, never offered any considerable resistance.

There were two principal routes of penetration. The one led down the Volkhov to Lake Ladoga, with the old Novgorodian settlement of Staraya Ladoga, and thence through the River Svir to Lake Onega. The other started down the upper course of the Volga, easily reached from Novgorod, and continued up some of its many tributaries which flow down from the north. From these various approaches the traders of Novgorod pushed on to the region "beyond the portages"—the *Zavolochie*, the basin of those great rivers, Onega, Northern Dvina, Pinega, and Mezen, which flow northwards to the White Sea.

Novgorod's trade and prosperity gained much from the occupation of the north. It produced furs in unlimited quantity. The upper course of the Vychega river (a tributary of the Northern Dvina) had salt mines, exploited by a great trading family, the Stroganovs, who penetrated by the same route to the Urals for various minerals. The northern towns of Vologda, Veliki Ustyug, Solvychegodsk and Solikamsk, owe their foundation to this period of colonisation.

Pskov, "the younger brother of Novgorod", was no less a city of commerce. But it suffered from a less convenient outlet to the Baltic, for after the passage through Lake Peipus to the Narova, the rapids in this river were an impassable obstruction, and transshipment was necessary to circumvent them. Pskov until the fourteenth century was a city subject to Novgorod, but it developed ambitions of independence, evolved its own constitution, which was more democratic than that of Novgorod, and in 1348 seceded from the parent state.

The earliest building surviving in Novgorod, and the only one of the eleventh century, is the Cathedral of St Sophia, built in the years 1045–52 by the son of Prince Yaroslav of Kiev. Its plan follows closely that of the St Sophia of Kiev, which was founded eight years earlier, and it was almost certainly the work of the same school of Greek architects. It is distinguished, however, from the cathedral of Kiev by a reduction in size, and by simplification in detail; although divided into five aisles, it has but three apses instead of five, and the mosaics of Kiev are replaced by frescoes. There is no marble, but some stone is used as well as brick, which is the most widespread and usually the only building material in Novgorod, as elsewhere in Russia. There are five cupolas crowned with bulbous domes over the main part of the church, and an additional dome at the west end, but the original ones were probably of different form. Externally, St Sophia shows little decoration. Simple shafts, running from top to bottom, decorate the apses at the eastern end, while broad pilaster-like projections on the north and south walls indicate the position of lines of vaulting. This expression on the outside walls of an internal structural feature is a very common character of the Novgorod churches, as of early Russian architecture in general [Plates 1, 2].

The history of architecture in Novgorod is mainly one of simplification. The humble dimensions and plainness of her churches is no doubt related to the fact that this was not a royal residence, but an essentially bourgeois town. However that may be, in the course of the twelfth, thirteenth and fourteenth centuries a progressive diminution in size can be followed, together with a reduction in the apses, and an almost entire loss of detail. In the Church of the Saviour, built at the end of the twelfth century, the two side apses are much reduced. In most churches of the thirteenth to fifteenth centuries they have completely disappeared, and the single central apse alone remains. In plan (p. 22) there is great uniformity. After the building of St Sophia, a plan so elaborate was never used again, perhaps because the Russian builders lacked the necessary technique. They kept to the simple square divided by four pillars into three aisles each made up of three vaults, from which followed an external division of all the walls into three arched spaces, the central arch being usually trifoliate [Plates 3, 4].

Besides these modifications, others appeared which were bound up with climatic conditions in northern Russia, and were possibly suggested by a German influence due to the close association of Novgorod with Lübeck and other Hanse towns. The prevalence of rain, and a very heavy winter snowfall, required the evolution of some new form of dome to replace the saucer-shaped form of the Byzantines, and of steep roofs to cover the external vaulting. Thus the later Novgorod churches are provided with two intersecting double-sloped roofs, giving a gable on each of the four sides. It is generally thought that such roofs, new to Russia at the time, came as a suggestion from Germany, though others claim them as manifesting an early influence of the native wooden architecture. That German masons did come to Novgorod is certain, and another new feature of the fourteenth and fifteenth-century churches—the blind arcade often encircling the apse—can hardly be explained except on the assumption of a German influence [Plate 4].[1]

The origin of the bulbous dome is an extremely controversial subject. That it was adopted from the Tartars is an old and impossible theory now quite abandoned, but several possible alternatives remain. Some form of dome that could throw off the snow in winter was absolutely required, and possibly the bulb was evolved directly from the Byzantine dome in response to this necessity. It is possible too that the bulb already existed in wooden architecture, and that this was the first of a long series of features borrowed from their native wooden style by the builders in brick and stone.

In any case, the bulb was either a creation or an adaptation by the Russians themselves, and there is conclusive evidence to show that it appeared in Novgorod some time during the twelfth century, long before the Tartars had any opportunity to introduce it. At least one writer believes that it was introduced into Russia from Poland with the baroque style. The fact that bulbous domes are actually represented in miniatures of the fourteenth century seems sufficient to dispose of this theory, even if it were credible that a feature so universal could have become so only since the seventeenth century.

In the churches of Novgorod and Vladimir it is possible roughly to trace an evolution in the shape of the Russian dome. Probably the earliest alteration of the Byzantine hemisphere was simply the addition

---

[1] Another curious feature of some Novgorod churches, doubtfully of foreign extraction, is the use of resonators (*golosnik*) in the form of earthenware pots imbedded in the walls, their mouths open to the interior.

of a cross. The next stage would have been the drawing out of the apex into a point, giving the so-called "helmet-shaped" dome (*shlem*), seen at Vladimir [Plates 9, 10] and in some churches at Novgorod. Later the sides of the dome were inflated, so as to overhang the drum below, producing the true bulb or onion (*luk*). This process was carried to excess in the seventeenth century. The duplicated cupolas common at Novgorod and elsewhere are presumably the result of subsequent and ill-judged alterations [Plates 3, 1; 4, 1].

The architecture of Pskov, though showing a general resemblance to that of Novgorod, diverged from it in some important ways, especially since Pskov became independent in the middle of the fourteenth century. Thus at Pskov certain new features appear, unknown at Novgorod. Closed galleries (*pápert*) are found, either at the west end or surrounding three sides of the church (D, p. 22), and covered stairways and porches (*kryltsó*) with curious dumpy pillars give access to them [Plate 6, 4].

Another original feature developed at Pskov was a system of construction by "encorbelled" or "superimposed" arches (C, p. 22). They were used as an alternative to the vault for the purpose of raising the cupola over a square base. Above four original arches resting on the sides of the square, further tiers were raised, each "corbelled out" inwards from the tier below, so gradually roofing in the space. These arches are visible only inside at Pskov, but when transplanted to Moscow their decorative value was quickly realised, and their form permitted to appear externally.

Further, at Pskov a new adjunct to the churches was developed in the fourteenth and fifteenth centuries. This was the *zvónnitsa* (French *clocher-arcade*). It is the earliest form of bell tower found in Russia, and its appearance coincides with the first introduction of real bells into the country; before that time a primitive gong of wood or metal (*bilo*) was the only kind of bell known. In the *zvónnitsa* of Pskov bells were hung under a series of arches arranged in a straight line, primitively two, later several, and in some later developments two tiers of arches are

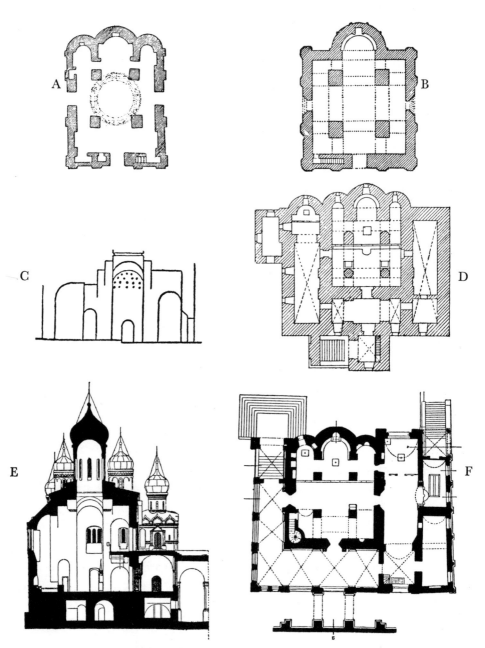

NOVGOROD, PSKOV, MOSCOW

NOVGOROD. A. Church of the Saviour (1198) showing three apses. B. Church of
the Transfiguration (1374); only one apse remains.

PSKOV. C. Diagrammatic longitudinal section of a church of the Pskov type,
showing the use of superposed or encorbelled arches. D. Plan of a church
(early fifteenth century) showing encircling galleries.

MOSCOW. E. Cathedral of the Annunciation (late fifteenth century) showing
system of vaulting exactly as in C. F. The same. Plan with galleries as in D.

found. This form of "bell cot" (the word tower seems inapplicable) spread to Novgorod; a good specimen stands adjacent to the Cathedral of St Sophia there. In the seventeenth century it was scattered all over Russia: both Rostov Veliki and Uglich have fine examples [Plates 6, 7].

By their escape from the Mongol invasion, Novgorod and Pskov remained the only part of Russia where building could flourish without interruption from the twelfth to the fifteenth century. In the early days of the new principality of Muscovy, architects from Pskov were freely employed both in Moscow itself and at Sergievo, for local craftsmen had by then quite lost the art of building. At this time the Pskov architects had a higher reputation than those of Novgorod, and Pskov was in any case more popular with Moscow, owing to a political policy more favourable to her, less independent and nationalistic than that of Novgorod. It therefore came about that Pskov was one of the several sources of inspiration for the new style of Moscow growing up in the early fifteenth century.

Few churches were built in Novgorod in the sixteenth century. Most are small, and single-domed. But the most interesting and picturesque is SS. Boris and Gleb, which has five domes, and a complex roof with many gables. It embodies "encorbelled arches" and was most probably the work of architects from Pskov (C, p. 22). All these sixteenth-century churches are characterised by flat pilasters on the outside walls, leading up to blind ogee arches;[1] their roofs are gabled, and their apses single [Plate 5].

From the second half of the fifteenth century onwards, there began the decadence of these north-western republics, a melancholy process which has continued with scarcely a relief ever since. It started with the secession of Novgorod's various northern colonies, and this the mother republic, with her feeble military organisation, was powerless to prevent. Moreover, the rising principality of Moscow saw only with concern the existence of independent states on her north-western

---

[1] Arches with a double curve, concave inside below, convex above, giving a tapering tip. *Ogival* has a different meaning, being applied to pointed arches in general.

frontiers. In 1478, Ivan III, Prince of Moscow, suppressed the *Véche* (Assembly) and the *Posádnik* (President) of Novgorod. In 1570, Ivan IV, well named "The Terrible", pillaged the town and massacred most of its inhabitants. The last blow to Novgorod came in the early eighteenth century with the foundation of St Petersburg, which meant the final deflection of all trade from the ancient commercial metropolis.

3. VLADIMIR

The region of the upper Volga, which was to emerge gradually in history as Muscovy, the new centre of all Russia, was populated by emigrants from the principality of Kiev on the Dnieper. There was a gradual streaming eastwards of this population during the eleventh and twelfth centuries. Its origin is reflected in many of the place-names, which repeat those of places in the Kiev country, or of its Princes; thus Vladimir and Yaroslavl, both founded in the eleventh century, were named after Vladimir and Yaroslav of Kiev.

In 1152 Prince Yuri Dolgoruki ("the long-armed") of Kiev, who had begun to take an interest in this eastern extension of his dominions, gave his name to Yuriev Polski ("George-town-in-the-Fields"). His successor, Andrey Bogolyubski, lost interest in the mother country, and moved his capital to Vladimir. Near by he established, and called by his own name, the village of Bogolyubovo, and there he built himself a palace, as well as a little church, one of the loveliest in Russia. In 1169, Andrey fell upon Kiev with his army and destroyed it. From then on, Novgorod was the only possible rival to Vladimir for supremacy in Russia, until the capital was moved to Moscow in the time of the "Tartar Yoke".

The history of architecture in this region owed much to its geographical orientation, which differed entirely from that of Kiev or Novgorod. It was more isolated from Byzantium than either of these cities, and, like Novgorod, was subject to other influences from abroad.

At Vladimir, however, these influences were eastern rather than western, for contacts with Asia, by way of the Volga, were much closer than with western Europe. It is generally thought that some of the most characteristic features of the Vladimir style were due to contact with the Caucasian region.

The architecture of Vladimir is unique in Russia, in that the material is not brick, but an excellent white sandstone, which was brought by water from distant quarries on the Kama. The plans are uniform and traditional, hardly differing from those of the smaller churches at Kiev and Novgorod (A–C, p. 31). The four walls of the square are each divided by long semi-columns into three, and from the eastern end there project three semicircular apses. These are beautifully ornamented with a blind arcade running round the top, of which every second or third column drops right down to the ground. The other sides of the church also carry an arcade at about their middle height. In the centre of the western, northern and southern façades are portals, recessed in several orders[1] and elaborately decorated [Plates 8–11].

All the decoration of these churches is carved in solid stone, in contrast to the stucco work usual in Russian architecture. The material itself invited sculpture, and this no doubt partly explains its lavish use. Russian sculpture of this period differs considerably from that of contemporary Romanesque architecture in western Europe. It is in flatter relief, and it tends to spread over all available surfaces, instead of being concentrated on particular structures. This character of the decoration links the architecture of Vladimir with that of the Caucasus, and as communications between these countries were easy, it is at least plausible to suggest a Caucasian influence on the Russian builders, who were always receptive to ideas from abroad.

But certain characters of the Vladimir style are more precisely associated by several writers with the architecture of Transcaucasia. Such are the beautiful arcades on the outside walls, and many of the actual

---

[1] The word applied to each simple arch, together with the pair of columns supporting it, in recessed doorways and other compound arches.

subjects of the carvings. The closest correspondence does certainly exist between the carvings of Vladimir and those of Akhtamar on Lake Van in southern Armenia; those of Pthni, near Erivan, can also be compared. On the other hand, it is equally true that the same subjects appear on many Romanesque churches of Lombardy and Tuscany, and types of arcade also occur here, which resemble those of Vladimir much more closely than do any in Armenia or Georgia. From contemporary records it seems that architects "from all countries" were employed at Vladimir, and there may well have been Italians among them. It is really impossible to decide which influence was dominant, but one need not ignore the possibility that both were operative.

The first church of the Vladimir epoch is the Cathedral of Pereyaslavl Zaleski (1152), but it is not very typical of the style. There followed in 1158 the Cathedral of the Assumption at Vladimir, though the present church is the result of rebuilding and considerable extension after a great fire in 1183. The extensions left it as a church with five aisles (not in any way connected with the five-aisled type of Kiev). Four extra domes were added on the corners, giving the five-domed arrangement which became so widespread in later centuries [Plate 9]. This cathedral was considered, until the fifteenth century, the greatest achievement of Russian architecture, and the first foreign architect imported to Moscow by Ivan III was sent to Vladimir to study it (see p. 30).

Of Vladimir churches the earliest remaining approximately in its original condition is that of the Intercession, built in 1165 near the village of Bogolyubovo. It is a replica in miniature of the first Cathedral of the Assumption, and probably the most perfect example of the Vladimir style. Both in itself, and in its very charming situation on the banks of the river Nerl, this is one of the most attractive specimens of architecture anywhere in Russia [Plate 8 and Frontispiece].

From 1195 dates the Church of St Dmitri, a larger and more elaborate edition of the "Intercession on the Nerl". Its walls above the arcade are smothered in sculptures, among which many subjects recall the art of the Sassanian Persians and other peoples of western Asia. Their

influence must have been felt at Vladimir, whether by way of Transcaucasian architecture, or otherwise [Plates 10–13].

Two well-known churches in the same region remain from the early
years of the thirteenth century: the cathedral of Suzdal, a five-domed
example, and the very remarkable church of Yuriev Polski. This latter,
differing somewhat in plan from the churches of Vladimir, excels them
all in the elaboration of its sculptured ornament, which originally
covered the entire surface of the walls, except at the eastern end. The
designs spread widely without regard to structural features, in a way
reminiscent of Transcaucasian or Mahommedan art, but scarcely represented in western Europe. The sculpture was apparently accom-
plished *in situ*, and in this respect differs from that of Vladimir itself,
where each stone bears a whole subject which was completed before
placing the stone in position. This church is the last monument of the
Vladimir style. It was built in 1234, only four years before the Mongols
overran the country, and architecture sank into abeyance for more than
a hundred years [Plates 14, 15].

This style of Vladimir, so successful and beautiful during its short
career of less than a hundred years, was suppressed in its prime by the
Mongol incursion of 1238. In this year all the towns of the upper Volga
and its tributaries—Suzdal, Rostov, Yaroslavl, Vladimir—were sacked
by the invaders. In due time, however, after two centuries of stagnation,
the surviving buildings of Vladimir were to play an important part in
the resuscitation of architecture under the Princes of Muscovy. They
provided the basic, if conservative element in a new style which was
freer from tradition and more characteristically Russian than any that
had gone before.

4. MOSCOW—THE BEGINNINGS

Mention is first made of Moscow in 1148, when it was a place of no great consequence, one of many settlements newly established by Yuri Dolgoruki. It takes its name from the little River Moskva, an affluent of the Oka, and thus in direct communication with the Volga itself. The river was not without importance, for it offered one good route from Novgorod to the great towns on the lower Volga. In later times Moscow gained rapidly in importance through its central position, from which radiated routes not only to the Baltic and the Caspian, but northwards to the White Sea, westwards to Poland through Smolensk, and southwards by way of the Don valley to the Black Sea (see map).

During the years of Tartar domination, the Russian Princes found it expedient to make themselves practically the vassals of the Khan, and to collect tribute for him from their much impoverished people. Ivan Kalita ("The Purse-bearer"), who cultivated the friendliest relations with his Tartar overlords, was by their favour styled "Grand Prince of Moscow", in the early part of the fourteenth century. Although Vladimir had hitherto remained technically the capital, and was still in fact the seat of the Russian Patriarch, Moscow had long outstripped it in importance. Ivan Kalita, with the Khan's support, made Moscow his political capital, and later (in 1328) transferred thither the patriarchal residence as well. He built the first church and the first Kremlin wall on what is still the Kremlin Hill at Moscow, and laid the foundations of that powerful principality of Muscovy, which was the nucleus of modern Russia.

The new state grew rapidly by the absorption of lesser neighbouring principalities. In time its Princes felt powerful enough to change their policy of submission to the Tartars for one of aggression. Under Ivan III (The Great), in 1480, central Russia was finally freed from Tartar domination. It was Ivan the Terrible who completed the task of liberation by his conquest of the Tartar Khanates of Kazan and Astrakhan in 1552 and 1554.

Some writers maintain that the Tartars' influence on Russian life and civilisation was good rather than bad, that they were tolerant of the Russian Church and did not interfere with the practice of the arts, religious or otherwise; further, that backward social customs (such as the inferior position of women) were an inheritance from Byzantine civilisation, by no means from the Tartars, who themselves were more advanced. Whatever the truth in these assertions, there can be no doubt as to the fate of architecture during the period in question. The country was impoverished, and building could not continue, even though not actively prevented. So when architectural activity was resumed during the rise of Moscow in the fourteenth and fifteenth centuries, the local population had almost lost the art of building, and the Princes of Moscow were obliged to send abroad and to north-west Russia for architects of technical skill commensurate with their larger undertakings.

One of the earliest churches marking the renaissance of architecture in the fourteenth century stands at Zvenígorod, a village to the west of Moscow. It evidently owes much inspiration to Vladimir, though generally simpler, and with differences in detail. Its plan and section can hardly be distinguished from those of St Dmitri and the Church of the Intercession at Vladimir (p. 31). As there, long round semi-columns divide the façades into three parts, and the three apses have a simple arcade with columns reaching to the ground. But the blind arcade which encircles three sides of the Vladimir churches is reduced here to a simple band of carved ornament [Plate 16].

A similar church of somewhat later date is that dedicated to the Nativity of the Virgin in the Savvino-Storozhevski Monastery near Zvenigorod. Its cupola and parts of the walls are covered with restored frescoes. The great monastery or *Lavra* of Sergievo, which was founded by St Sergius during the reign of Ivan Kalita, contains a Cathedral of the Trinity belonging to the same type, and similarly painted outside [Plate 17].

These small churches were no doubt built by Russian, though perhaps not by local, architects. But when, in the fifteenth century, Ivan III decided to erect several large cathedrals in the Kremlin at Moscow, Russian architects proved unequal to the task; their churches collapsed in the course of construction, and Ivan fell back on foreign help. He might well have applied to the Germans and Scandinavians already established in the north-west at Novgorod. Actually he turned to Italy, the decisive factor in his choice being no doubt the counsel of his almost Italian wife, Zoë Palaeologus, for, though a Byzantine Princess by birth, she had been educated in Rome. There were, however, other connections with Italy, for Italians from Venice and Genoa had now supplanted the Greeks in the monopoly of trade with Russia through the Black Sea. Their chief trading base was Caffa on the eastern coast of the Crimea, and from here the trade route followed up the Don Valley towards Moscow, just as, starting from Cherson, it had formerly followed the Dnieper to Kiev.

Nothing remains of Ivan Kalita's fourteenth-century Kremlin except the little Church of the Saviour "in the forest", surrounded no longer by trees, but by the high walls of palaces which hide it completely from view. The Kremlin as it now appears is largely the work of Italians imported by Ivan III. They built not only the two larger cathedrals, but the main part (other than the towers) of the present Kremlin wall, and also the *Granovitaya Palata*, a "facetted" *palazzina* in pure Renaissance style.

One Aristotle Fioraventini was the first Italian architect to be imported into Russia by Ivan III. He was sent to Vladimir to study the Cathedral of the Assumption there, and instructed to build a church of the same type, to be given the same dedication, within the Kremlin walls at Moscow. He did not faithfully reproduce the prototype of Vladimir, but lengthened the plan, provided five apses instead of three, and reduced the number of aisles from five to three (C, D, E, p. 31). His higher technical skill in building is reflected in the comparatively small area covered by the supporting columns, and this gives a more roomy impression to the interior than is usual in Russian churches [Plates 18, 47].

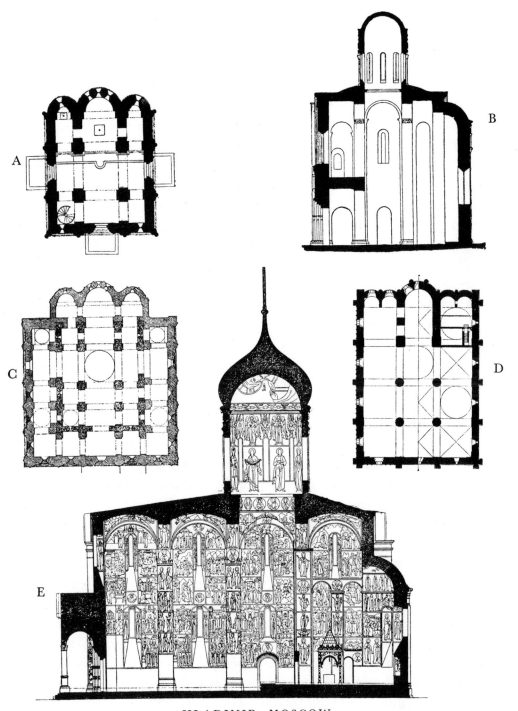

VLADIMIR, MOSCOW

VLADIMIR. A. Plan of St Dmitri. B. Longitudinal section of the church of the Intercession at Bogolyubovo. The earliest churches of Moscow closely resemble these both in plan and section. C. Cathedral of the Assumption.

MOSCOW. D. Cathedral of the Assumption. Horizontal section at two different levels; the position of the domes is shown on the right half. The plan of this cathedral was based fundamentally on that of the Assumption at Vladimir. E. The same. Longitudinal section showing the frescoes.

The little Cathedral of the Annunciation was built in the years
1482–90 by architects from Pskov [Plate 19]. Though the smallest, it
is undoubtedly the most picturesque of the three cathedrals in the
Kremlin. In this church one finds used with marked decorative success
the "superimposed" or "encorbelled" arches (*kokóshnik*), evolved by
the architects of Pskov. They are arranged on exactly the same principle as in SS. Boris and Gleb at Novgorod, also the work of Pskov
architects (C, p. 22). These *kokoshniki* met with tremendous popularity
in the later architecture of Moscow, but soon began to be used exclusively as decoration, losing their original function; moreover,
through the influence (perhaps already operative in the Cathedral of
the Annunciation) of the *bochka*[1] used in wooden architecture, *kokoshniki*
later assumed a great variety of new forms. This cathedral shows also
external galleries and covered stairways of the type already familiar
to the architects in their home town. (Compare the very similar plans
of this and a Pskov church at D and F, p. 22.)

Lastly, one must refer to the Cathedral of the Archangel Michael,
burial place of the Tsars before Peter the Great, and a building
of great significance in the history of Russian architecture [Plates 20;
51, 2]. Like the Assumption, it was the work of Italians, of whom a
continuous stream had been brought to Moscow from 1474 onwards.
This, the third of the Kremlin cathedrals, was built early in the
sixteenth century. The plan and general appearance are traditional,
but various details, drawn from the Italian Renaissance style, are here
used for the first time in Russia, where they immediately became very
popular. The outside walls have pilasters in two tiers, each carrying a
cornice; above the upper of these are conchs filling the arched spaces
provided by the vaulting of the roof. Decorative details, disposed
around windows and doorways, and on the bases and capitals of pilasters,
include acanthus leaves and other formalised vegetable subjects. The
novel features so much admired and so readily copied were the heavy
cornice running round under the roof, and the row of semicircular

[1] See pp. 36–7.

spaces above it. These semicircles, generally without the shells, were very widely used; they were made to fit in with and lead up to the tiers of *kokoshniki* above.

Thus it will be seen that Muscovite architecture of the fifteenth century was a composite creation, owing much to Italy, especially in the actual technique of building, and in ornament, and much also to Pskov; but yet following in its general characters the plan laid down at Vladimir in the twelfth century. A new influence, more powerful than these, began to be felt in the early sixteenth century, and made at last of Russian architecture something really national, showing but little trace of its Byzantine origin. This influence came from the wooden architecture of the north, a truly native style of building unconnected, as far as is known, with anything outside Russia. Before going on to describe the further development of the Muscovite style, one must digress to contemplate this peasant art of the northern forests, certainly one of the most attractive and interesting subjects in the whole field of Russian architecture.

5. WOODEN ARCHITECTURE UP TO THE SIXTEENTH CENTURY

When studying wooden architecture, the point of view cannot be the same as that from which one approaches stone and brick building. In their case, the actual age of every building is a question of fundamental importance. The material being durable, specimens of such architecture generally survive from all ages in numbers sufficient to make possible a history based on direct evidence. With wood it is different.

In north Russia practically no wooden buildings remain from the period now in question. Two beautiful churches have been shown, indeed, to date from the last year of the sixteenth century; one of these was destroyed by fire before even the second became known, for the latter was brought to light only a few years ago in a remote part of the province of Archangel. Remains of earlier date are extremely scanty.

One explanation is the terrible frequency of fires in Russia. Villages are periodically burnt, and for this reason churches were often built at a distance from them. Even so, their chance of survival for more than two or three hundred years was extremely small.

There are, of course, wooden buildings in some countries of much earlier date than any remaining in Russia. The survival of a few wooden churches in Norway from the twelfth century is an extraordinary fact, and unexplained.[1] In other cases, however, such survival, as of many wooden buildings in this country, is explained by the use of oak or other woods naturally more resistant than fir and pine, which are the invariable material in Russia. Nevertheless, these woods are harder where they grow in the northern part of the country than they are further south, a fact which partly accounts for the higher percentage of survival among churches in the far north.

In Russia, therefore, one cannot build up a history of early wooden architecture from a consecutive series of dated examples. One can only arrange existing buildings in series according to their type, without regard to actual chronology. That such a series represents a real historical sequence cannot definitely be proved, but all the evidence suggests that this is so. There is no doubt that some sort of wooden architecture existed as early as the introduction of Christianity into Russia. At a slightly later time actual buildings are recorded, as for instance the first Cathedral of St Sophia in Novgorod, which was constructed in 989, and burnt early in the eleventh century.

The ordinary peasants' dwellings (*izbá*), such as have been built for centuries in Russia on practically the same plan, and are still so built, represent a fairly primitive form of wooden building. The most elementary type of all, however, is found in the village bath houses. Here is Russian wooden architecture in its simplest possible form, unobscured by any attempts at elaboration or embellishment, and one may plausibly

[1] A "Bishop's Palace" of similar age in the Faroe Islands has remained because of the extraordinary hardness of the timber, which was drift wood seasoned by years of exposure.

imagine that the earliest wooden dwellings in Russia were something of this kind.

They are simple rectangles, the walls built of round logs laid horizontally, and intersecting at the corners. Each log is somewhat hollowed on the lower surface, so as to fit down over the one below, and between them is wedged some kind of caulking or packing, which goes far to make the walls proof against air and moisture. The simple gabled roof is covered with long overlapping boards, or with shingles. This system of construction with horizontal timbers, described by Strzygowski as "block-work", has always been universal in the Slav countries, and remains so among the peasantry. Uprights, such as corner posts, are unknown. While these houses are being built, they rise gradually from the ground, as layer on layer of horizontal logs is added to the framework. Certainly a wasteful system, but timber was always plentiful in Russia, and formerly much more so than now.

In the felling of trees, and in the building of *izby* and churches, the Russian carpenters used but a single implement—the common hand axe. Saws were unknown until the eighteenth century, but even now, when they are available, the peasant carpenters prefer to stick to the traditional axe, in the use of which they have acquired uncommon skill.

No doubt the first Christian churches and chapels in Russia were of the primitive rectangular type. But at some stage, one cannot know even approximately when, or how, a new form came into being—the octagon. It seems that this form was used exclusively for religious purposes: it is never seen in ordinary secular buildings. Since the appearance of the octagon, two main lines of evolution must have been followed, one based on the rectangular, the other on the polygonal plan. These two types existed side by side, and many specimens of both remain from the seventeenth century; only a very few from earlier times.

Churches of the rectangular tradition were evolved by the juxtaposition in a straight line of several frameworks. The basic framework, a square or oblong box without any additions or appurtenances, is expressed by three or four words in Russian, but no equivalent exists in English. An *izba* commonly consists of one element, though it may be divided up to any extent inside [Plate 66, 1]. The most usual form of church has three, of which the central one is the largest, and corresponds to the body of the church, while the other two, added to the east and west ends, are respectively the sanctuary (containing the altar) and a kind of vestibule (*trápeza* or *pritvór*), corresponding to the narthex of Byzantine and Romanesque churches. In this type of church the central compartment was usually given a very steep "wedge-shaped" roof, crowned by a small bulbous dome covered with shingles [Plate 67, 2]. At a distance, this gives an impression very similar to the "tent-roof" (*shatyór*) of the churches next to be described, and no doubt to some extent satisfied the popular fancy for a high conical roof, a taste which must have been deeply implanted in the Russian people.

The other type of church, based on the octagonal plan, is more interesting and more striking. It is the most original and captivating creation of the Russians in the whole province of architecture. The tiny octagon in its primitive form, as it can still be seen, is humble enough [Plate 66, 2]. But this led on to greater things. If the eight walls of such a small octagon be carried on upwards, but allowed to converge gradually until they meet at a point, the result is a tapering cone, hardly "tent-shaped", as the Russian name implies, but something like a spire. Probably the tent-roof of the Russian wooden churches was produced almost of itself in this way. It is built on exactly the same principle as the walls, except that the logs, lying horizontally tier on tier, are not so closely applied, and are finally covered over with overlapping boards or scale-like shingles. At the tip of the cone is always placed a little onion-dome [Plate 68].

As in those of rectangular plan, the central element of the "tent" church, this time an octagon with tapering roof, is adjoined east and west by lesser compartments: these may be square, or the eastern one may be apsidiform and facetted (A, p. 65). The two projections may be covered by a ridged roof, in section like an ogee or a pointed horseshoe, ending in a gable. This is the *bóchka* or cask. The floor is generally at some height above the ground, for the sake of dryness, and to avoid the snow, which may lie very deeply in winter. To meet the need for an approach to the church, a double stairway with balustrades and roof was almost always added at the western end, and sometimes made the object of elaborate ornamentation, while the rest of the church remained plain.[1] Often a covered gallery or balcony, a few feet above ground and adjoining the stairway, runs round the western part of the church [Plate 69].

Inside, one sees nothing of the great conical roof. A low ceiling, sometimes scarcely above head level, cuts off from view the whole upper region of the church (B, p. 65). This is probably necessitated by the demand for warmth in winter. There is, however, a total lack of relationship between the outside and the inside of these buildings. Architectural impressiveness is never attempted inside. Not that the interiors are uninteresting, but they give no suggestion of the originality and variety displayed outside. From the upper platform of the *kryltso*, meeting place of the two stairways, one enters a vestibule or *trapeznaya*, which in turn gives access to the church proper. *Trapeznaya* (or *trapeza*) is the word applied to the refectory of a monastery; it implies a space set aside, if not for eating in particular, at least for secular purposes generally. And the *trapeznaya* of a church, furnished and lit like an ordinary peasants' *izba*, was a place where the congregation, which had often come long distances for some special church function, could gather socially, eat and drink, and, on occasion, spend the night. To provide for occasions when a large congregation could not all find room in the church proper, the walls dividing it from the *trapeznaya* were pierced with long slits, giving a view through to the altar. The central part of the church is entirely different. Dark and bare, except for the gilded *iconostas* with its tiers of icons, drawing forward the eyes of the

---

[1] This covered stairway (*kryltsó*) occurs also in domestic buildings, and may have been adopted from them. Even the humblest *izba* may have one, but the stairway, in this case, is more often single.

congregation towards the altar, this space was calculated to create a fitting atmosphere for the celebration of religious rites.

Though the earliest known churches of the "tent-roofed" type date from 1600, there can be no question that they existed long before. One of the two examples definitely dating from that year, a magnificent specimen discovered and studied by Professor Baranovski, shows the type in full perfection; it is obviously the end-product of a long period of evolution.

Another form of church must have evolved in the course of the six-teenth century. It has a cruciform plan, for the central division is ad-joined by extra compartments on all four sides, not only to east and west, and each carries its twisted roof or *bochka* [Plate 73, 1]. A variant of this type shows the ridges of the *bochka* shortened so that hardly more than the gable is left, and in this form they can stand in two or even three tiers [Plate 73, 2]. The arrangement is of interest on account of its supposed influence on brick architecture (see pp. 40 and 63).

Bell towers cannot have appeared very early in north Russia, for there were no bells to be housed in them until the fifteenth century. At that time, however, a wooden bell tower is recorded as existing in Nov-gorod, and probably it was not long before they spread all over the north, and assumed the characteristic form which is still found there. Their form is primitively octagonal from the ground upwards. On top of the octagon is a circlet of short columns carrying the conical roof, and housing the bells themselves [Plate 80]. These bell towers were always separate from the churches, for churches were evolved, as entities com-plete in themselves, long before the need for bell towers arose, and the problem of how satisfactorily to unite them was difficult. Not until the end of the seventeenth century were combined types evolved, and these seldom give an effect as completely pleasing as the older arrangement. Many of the north Russian *pogosty*[1] with their churches, chapels and bell tower grouped without system or symmetry, have a quite extraordinary charm, like a place dreamt of, or imagined in a fairy tale.

[1] *Pogóst*—a cemetery containing churches.

It is generally believed that many of the features of this national wooden architecture were incorporated, in the early sixteenth century, into the growing Muscovite style, at that time particularly receptive to new ideas. This subject will be referred to again, and mention made also of other theories which would deprive the wooden style of its importance either as originator or as transmitter of new architectural features.

The evolution of the northern wooden style was by no means at an end with the appearance of the great "tent" churches. On the contrary, it experienced a very remarkable expansion in the seventeenth and eighteenth centuries. But since these later developments can have had no effect on the evolution of brick architecture, but were themselves influenced by it, and since an account of them would here be chronologically out of place, the subject will be deferred to the last chapter of this outline.

6. THE MUSCOVITE STYLE BEFORE 1650

The great expansion of Russian architecture on new and original lines which took place at the beginning of the sixteenth century was the result of several circumstances operating together. Muscovy was now an independent and growing state, liberated not only from the domination of Tartar overlords, but also from the ecclesiastical authority of Constantinople, since the capture of that city by the Turks in 1453. Moscow had become the capital of the only independent country adhering to the Eastern Church; the one metropolis of Orthodoxy; the successor of Byzantium and the "Third Rome". The feeling of power and independence consequent on these two events must have been favourable to originality in architecture. In any case, this period saw an entirely new departure, involving almost complete abandonment of the Byzantine tradition in building.

The monuments of this class are unfortunately few. Most of them are found in the surroundings of Moscow, and in Moscow itself stands the

famous end-product of one tendency in the style—the fantastic Cathedral of St Basil in the Red Square, probably the best known church in
all Russia, and one of the few carrying some reputation abroad.

In general character these churches are distinguished by the adoption,
instead of the Byzantine dome or group of domes, of a central "tent"
roof, and of several other features derived from the wooden architecture
of north Russia. Owing to their tall, attenuated form, they are known
as "pillar-" or "tower-shaped" churches.

The earliest example (1529) is a church dedicated to the Beheading
of John the Baptist at Dyakovo [Plate 22, 1]. It has not whole-heartedly
adopted the conical form of the "tent" churches, for its central element
does not taper to a point but ends bluntly in a somewhat depressed
dome. The four lesser elements surrounding the central one are similar
in form, and arranged at the four corners of the central structure.
Though a real "tent" is wanting, the separate elements of this church
have a good deal in common with some wooden types. The arrangement
of four smaller structures at the corners of the central tower has not,
however, any known prototype in wood, and was perhaps suggested by
the traditional disposition of the five domes in brick churches.

Not far from the church of Dyakovo stands another in which the
wooden "tent" tower is translated into stone with but little change.
This is the church of Kolomenskoe, dedicated to the Ascension [Plate
22, 2]. In the Russian books it is commonly found illustrated along
with the wooden church of Varzuga on the Kola peninsula, and a close
comparison is made between the superimposed *bochki* of the one, and
similar structures repeated in brick in the other. (Una [Plate 73, 2]
resembles Varzuga.) It is pointed out that although the brick church
was built some time before its "prototype", the latter probably inherits
the characters of a succession of earlier churches built on the same plan,
of which some would have preceded any appearance of the type in
brick. Other features at Kolomenskoe, unquestionably taking after
wooden prototypes, are these: the substructure (*podklet*) raising the actual
church to a height above the ground; the gallery surrounding the church

on three sides, and the covered stairways leading to it (A, p. 42). At the same time this building displays great originality in the disposition of its parts. Many of the details are distinctively Italian, and some consider that the architect was of that race, but there is no conclusive evidence on the subject.

A third church of similar type, standing, like the other two, overlooking the valley of the Moskva river, is the Transfiguration at Ostrovo, built in 1550. Here, adjacent to a central conical tower resembling that of Kolomenskoe, there were applied two subsidiary structures crowned with bulbous domes. The building is freely provided with *kokoshniki* of various forms, of which seven tiers adorn the central tower alone; but they are purely decorative, and have no relation to structure [Plate 23].

These three buildings served as prototypes for the extraordinary Church of Vasili Blazhenny ("Basil the Blessed") in the Red Square at Moscow [Plates 24 and 25]. This building is often described as the most typical example of the Russian style. But it is typical in no sense at all; it is, on the contrary, the only such church in the whole country; an oddity, almost a caricature. Whether or not for the legendary reason, that Ivan the Terrible blinded his architects to prevent any repetition of their work, nothing like it was ever seen again in Russia, or anywhere else in the world. Ivan the Terrible built the church between the years 1555 and 1560 to commemorate the conquest of Kazan.

A tall "tent" surmounting an octagonal base forms the central element of this complicated building, and around it are clustered eight more tower-like chapels crowned with massive bulbous domes variously decorated and coloured (plan, B, p. 42). The whole building is a world in itself of towers and domes, with an extraordinary profusion of decorative *kokoshniki* and every conceivable form of ornamental excrescence picked out in a brilliant and varied colour scheme. It is no wonder that many travellers and authors have exhausted their descriptive vocabulary in the effort to portray so unique a structure.

Yet a little understanding of the origin of its various forms enables

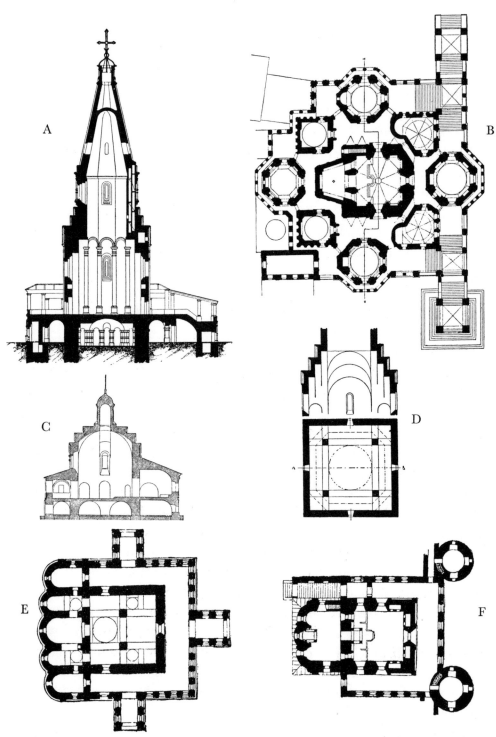

MOSCOW, YAROSLAVL, ROSTOV

MOSCOW. A. Section of the church at Kolomenskoe. B. Plan of St Basil. C. Longitudinal section of the Church of the Intercession showing purely ornamental *kokoshniki*. D. Church of the Nativity; plan and section of one of the towers, showing structural *kokoshniki*.

YAROSLAVL. E. Typical plan (St John the Baptist).

ROSTOV VELIKI. F. Typical fortress church with defensive towers (St John Theologos).

one to take a calmer and more objective view of the building. As Mrs Newmarch[1] says:

Undoubtedly, to those who know nothing of "wooden Russia" it is hopelessly enigmatical, a kind of weird, rootless architectural toadstool;...but to Russians who can link it with a long line of wooden ancestors, it appears less abnormal, less a law unto itself.

The genesis of the church itself involved, indeed, a wooden period, for the ring of outer chapels were originally of this material, to be replaced a few years later in brick.

In the descriptive literature on "St Basil" comparisons with the vegetable world are frequent. Alfred Maskell[2] wrote:

That it can be a church seems an impossibility. It seems rather to be some monstrous vegetable production, a fantastic dream, a Chinese puzzle. Yet the capriciousness of its very eccentricity is to some extent pleasing. One marvels if one does not admire.

Réau remarks:

L'église à la fois une et multiple surgit au fond de la Place Rouge comme une gerbe de neuf fleurs multicolores jaillissant d'une même tige.

But Théophile Gautier was otherwise impressed. To him it suggested "a stalactite grotto turned upside down".

With some, the only reaction is one of repulsion almost amounting to horror. It is said that Napoleon ordered the destruction of "that mosque"; it was preserved, however, as a convenient lodging for some of his troops. Yet Napoleon was not insensitive to the beauties of architecture; he is said to have given special orders to preserve the baroque Church of the Assumption, at that time quite a new building in Moscow [Plate 58, 2]. Fergusson, whose power of appreciation he had himself poisoned by the elaboration of inflexible "principles of beauty", described the church as "a combination of as much barbarity as it is

[1] In *The Russian Arts.*

[2] South Kensington Museum Art Handbook: *Russian Art and Art Objects in Russia*, 1884.

possible to bring together in so small a space", and in similar terms he wrote of Russian architecture in general.

In spite of these criticisms, there are many, especially among those who have lived with it in Moscow, who love and admire the Church of Vasili Blazhenny beyond all others. And those who know it less intimately may find, when their first impression of chaos and "barbarity" has passed away, that a rare beauty of proportion emerges from apparent confusion, and that an impression of tranquillity is left with them, not one of chaos. The peculiar beauty of this church emerges especially if one contemplates it from a little distance, and some happy play of sun or moonshine gives it for a passing moment a new being, unthought of before.

St Basil at Moscow, like its prototype of Dyakovo, is a combination of almost separate elements connected only at the base. Another type of brick tent-roofed church consists of a single base planned on the conventional quadrangle, but surmounted by two or three "tents" replacing the cupolas of Byzantine tradition. A fine specimen exists at Uglich. Here two smaller side "tents" are built in subjection to a larger one in the middle, and all three stand on separate octagonal bases, as in the wooden churches of the north [Plate 28, 2; and cf. Plate 72].

Later examples, of which a few exist in Moscow and elsewhere, are degenerate in that the separate bases are lost, and the towers become purely decorative, being simply added to a vaulted roof already complete in itself. Some of these churches have two tents. There is one at Nizhni Novgorod [Plate 28, 3], and another stood formerly on the site of the huge Cathedral of the Redeemer in Moscow, which has in turn been abolished to make way for a Palace of the Soviets.

Other churches of this type have three tents, and of these the most remarkable by far is the little Church of the Nativity in Moscow [Plate 29]. Here one may well excuse any theoretical defects in design and enjoy only the picturesque irregularity of the plan, and the profusion of decoration in which tent towers and tiers of *kokoshniki*, Italian cornices and conchs are all most happily combined. One of the towers (that on the left in Plate 29) is built up on three tiers of *kokoshniki* which, without being essential to the structure, are not merely moulded in the substance of the vault, as usually happens when *kokoshniki* become decorative. As may be seen from the section and plan on p. 42 (D), the vault actually rises in three steps by means of the corbelling out of arches. But these are not entirely self-supporting, nor do they of themselves carry the turret above; four internal pillars are provided to assist in both functions.

This charming church, built between 1649 and 1652, was the last outburst of the truly Russian style of the first half of the seventeenth century. In 1650 came the fateful edict of the Patriarch, practically prohibiting the erection of tent-roofed churches, and relegating this favourite feature to bell towers and subsidiary buildings. But for this crippling action of the Church, damning all original forms as contrary to tradition, the architecture of Russia might have produced monuments far more striking than anything we actually have. As it was, the ecclesiastical authorities attempted architectural standardisation, and laid down that churches should have a square plan with Greek cross inscribed, and five domes arranged in the traditional pattern.

There were, of course, other churches of this period, including some, such as the principal church of the Novodevichi Monastery in Moscow, and the cathedral of Rostov Veliki, following the pattern of the Kremlin cathedrals [Plate 21, 1, 2]. Another, and more interesting because more original type, has an early representative in the old *sobor* of the Don Monastery on the southern outskirts of Moscow [Plate 26]. It has but a single central cupola, surmounting several rows of *kokoshniki*, giving the general outline of a pyramid springing from the four walls of the church. It was built at the end of the sixteenth century. Several others of the same general character occur among Moscow churches of the early seventeenth century [Plate 27]. Their *kokoshniki* are non-structural, being simply built up on top of a massive cross-vault (section, C, p. 42).

Although a wooden origin for most of the new architectural features of this period—*bochki*, tent towers, galleries, covered stairways—has been accepted for some time, theories are not wanting that would ascribe to them a quite different origin, and even make the brick forms prototypes of those in wood. According to such theories, the conical towers would be poor copies of west European church steeples, transmitted finally to the wooden churches of the north. The fact that almost all existing wooden specimens are, in fact, subsequent, may appear at first sight to support the argument, but it does not really do so. Wooden buildings necessarily decay and vanish, and a little imagination is not only permissible, but essential for their reconstruction. Moreover, it is a principle of worldwide application that wooden architecture, which preceded stone in time, always tended to influence the forms produced in more durable material. Naturally this influence must be strongest when architecture is in a formative period, lacking potentialities of its own, as was Russian architecture in the early sixteenth century. On the whole, the wooden theory seems likely to hold the field.

The next phase in the history of Russian architecture shows that in spite of the unfortunate interference of a high-handed Church, potentiality enough was left to allow of a tremendous expansion, and the appearance of some of the finest specimens of Russian art existing. The second half of the seventeenth century was the period of greatest church-building activity the country has ever known.

7. THE NATIONAL STYLE OF MOSCOW AND YAROSLAVL SINCE 1650

The final period in the history of Russian architecture properly so-called (excepting the northern wooden style, which persisted longer) coincides with the second half of the seventeenth and the first 20 years of the eighteenth centuries. During this period the baroque style of central Europe filtered in from the countries on Russia's western frontier, and, towards the end of the century, it took Moscow by storm; the resulting style is known as Muscovite baroque, and is separately described. It is not really possible, however, to draw a sharp line between the earlier, more distinctively Russian buildings, and the later ones which are properly described as baroque. There was no abrupt transition, but a gradual change occurred in the character of surface decoration. Most of the buildings here to be mentioned do show, in some degree, a western influence.

Some of the finest buildings of the period are those of Yaroslavl, which in the latter part of the seventeenth century became a serious rival to Moscow for supremacy in the architectural world. At Yaroslavl, the baroque influx which so greatly modified the architecture of Moscow had little effect, and the genuine Russian style survived longer. It is indeed here at Yaroslavl, and not at Moscow, that the climax is reached of Russian architectural development.

Practically every church since the middle of the seventeenth century, and before the coming of the baroque, carries its sacred complement of five domes in the orthodox pattern. But these domes, with their supporting drums, have usually become a mere ornament perched on top of a roof which is structurally complete without them; they are blind, or "deaf" as the Russians say. It is indeed curious to reflect that these cupolas are the lineal descendants of the low drums and saucer domes of the Byzantines. The drums are drawn out into mere chimneys, carrying at their tips small but much inflated domes whose highly painted surfaces are spread over a metal framework, like cloth on the frame of an umbrella.

Yet some of these churches give a very pleasing effect. In Moscow itself is the Church of the "Georgian Mother of God", built in 1653 [Plate 32]. Here the transition from the walls through several rows of ogee *kokoshniki* to the slender cupolas is effected very beautifully, and the adventitious nature of the *kokoshniki* is less obvious than usual. In this church the groups of pilasters on the outside walls bear some relation to the actual vaulting, and the *kokoshniki* are so arranged that if they were structural, their weight would actually rest on the heads of pilasters. Moreover, there is a fine porch with conical roof and arches with pendants, a very popular if theoretically inartistic feature.

The most elaborate of all the later Moscow churches is that of Ostankino a few miles to the north of the town [Plate 33]. Here decoration has quite foregone its connection with structure, and the cupolas are even more grotesquely attenuated. Nekrasov, always quick to detect "degeneracy", writes as follows:

[In such churches] there remain as architectural lines (that is, lines defining the structure of the building) only the corners, foundations, and tops of the walls; in other words the church presents itself as an undifferentiated cube like the wooden *klet*,[1] on which flights of windows and other decorative details are spread arbitrarily. The kokoshniki...have entirely lost their original meaning. They are not only cut off from the walls by cornices, but their numbers often fail to correspond with the divisions of the wall, so that the springings of the kokoshniki come to lie not over pilasters, but over blank wall or even windows.

The wooden influence shows itself more particularly in the porches and galleries attached to these churches, the former often with conical or pyramidal roofs, which also invariably adorn the bell towers which became extremely popular at this time. At the village of Taininskoe near Moscow is a church with elaborate covered stairways very reminiscent of those occurring in wooden architecture, together with a *bochka* indistinguishable in form from those of the wooden churches [Plate 31].

A novel feature of the period is the combination of church and bell tower, the tower being generally placed at the western extremity of the church, but separated from the main square of the plan by a lower connecting building, often serving as a narthex or vestibule. This is so with the church at Ostankino. Other hardly less striking examples are St Nicholas in the district of Khamovniki, and St Gregory of Neocaesarea (1679) [Plate 30].

The most distinctive decorative novelty in these more elaborate Moscow churches is seen in the windows, which have little pediments of very curious form; they are presumably an expression of baroque

[1] Primitive rectangular framework.

influence, though not of the same shape as those which came later. Elaborate brick decoration is freely used in Moscow as in Yaroslavl, and is applied especially to the jambs[1] and archivolts[2] of doors and windows. The most popular motive in this brickwork consists in a succession of swellings giving the effect of a string of beads. Its origin is almost certainly to be found in wood carving. Porches and other entrance ways are elaborately ornamented. They often have peculiar "pitcher-shaped" pillars, while the arches are provided with one or two, even sometimes three pendants, hanging without support [Plate 31, 4; 53, 4].

Besides the larger churches already mentioned, there are hosts of lesser ones in a somewhat simplified style, not only in Moscow but in every provincial town. Most of these dispense with *kokoshniki*, and the cupolas emerge, rather inartistically it must be admitted, through the steep roof which covers and protects the vaulting [Plate 30, 1, 2; 34, 1]. Often the most attractive part of such churches is their tall conical bell tower, for this was a really popular feature; as such it evoked more attention from the architect, and escaped the commonplaceness of the church itself.

About the middle of the seventeenth century a number of provincial towns lying along the upper Volga began to rival Moscow in the artistic world; such were Uglich, Romanovo-Borisoglebsk, and, especially, Yaroslavl, together with Rostov "the Great" on the road between Yaroslavl and Moscow.

The pre-eminence of Yaroslavl came from its position at the crossing of two major trade routes of that time—the Volga route to the Caspian, and the highway between Vologda and Moscow. The latter was an essential link in the route to and from the White Sea, which had assumed

---

[1] The sides of a door or window, often consisting (as in wooden buildings) of single vertical members, but in brick architecture simply an area of brickwork generally singled out for elaborate decoration.

[2] The exposed surface of the arch above an opening. Like the jamb, this is constantly made the subject of decorative treatment.

tremendous importance as the only unobstructed outlet from Muscovy to western Europe. In summer thousands of barges were towed by man-power up the River Dvina from Archangel to Veliki Ustyug, and thence by way of the Sukhona to Vologda. Here the goods were stored on land until winter, when they were drawn over the snow in sledges through Yaroslavl, Rostov and Sergievo to Moscow.

The splendid churches of Yaroslavl, mostly built by wealthy merchants from their private resources, form a class apart from those of Moscow. Their size alone is unusual, and in this they eclipse all others in Russia. Their cupolas (at least, the central ones) are not false, but have perforated drums admitting light to the interior. Their most distinctive character is, however, the closed gallery (*papert*) encircling the church on three sides, and the magnificent porches giving access to it; also the two side chapels at the east end, each giving an additional apse to the eastern façade (plan, E, p. 42). Peculiar to the architecture of Yaroslavl is the elaborate panelled brickwork, and the decoration in faience round the eastern windows; in common with Moscow it has richly carved doors, and arches with pendants.

One of the earliest churches is St John Chrysostom, completed in 1654. The two projecting chapels at the eastern end are crowned with tent-shaped towers. The spacious outside gallery has huge porches, whose arches show one or two pendants apiece. Adjoining is a magnificent belfry, plain below, but highly ornamented above. It is one of the tallest of its kind [Plates 35, 36].

Of all Yaroslavl churches the most brilliant and striking is St John the Baptist, built in 1671–87 at Tolchkovo, a little distance from the town [Plates 37–9, 1]. The side chapels each carry an extra group of five cupolas, making in all a forest of no less than fifteen brilliantly gilded domes which blaze flame-like in the sunshine. The walls of church and gallery, and the three fine entrance porches, are resplendent in intricate brickwork built up in panels round nuclei of coloured tiles. Inside the gallery, as also in the body of the church, one finds walls and vault completely smothered in brightly coloured frescoes [Plates 40, 41].

The Church of Peter and Paul (1691), picturesquely perched on the high bank of the Volga, has a painted eastern end with windows encased by coloured faience [Plate 39, 2]. In other respects this late example shows a falling off in quality when compared with the foregoing.

Some of the outbuildings of these Yaroslavl sanctuaries are quite as attractive as the churches themselves. Adjoining the Church of St Nicholas is an exquisite semi-detached porch with brick and tile work in panels and nicely proportioned conical roof [Plate 43, 2]. As delightful are some of the "Holy Gates" giving access through an encircling wall to the precincts of these churches. An example is that of St John the Baptist at Yaroslavl [Plate 43, 1]; a still taller one of similar form leads into the cathedral enclosure at Romanovo-Borisoglebsk [Plate 44, 2].

Of other towns in this region, Uglich has fine churches with combined bell towers, often built over the entrance way [Plate 44, 3]. Uglich is a town whose glory has departed, a remote and sleepy place; formerly it could claim a dozen monasteries and more than 150 churches. Its fine "tent" church has already been mentioned; it contains also a small red-brick building of the fifteenth century, which is almost the only specimen of domestic architecture remaining in Russia from that period [Plate 63, 1]. It was here that the young Dmitri, Ivan the Terrible's son by his fifth wife, was murdered in 1591—by order, it is generally thought, of Boris Godunov. One of the many churches of Uglich stands on the site of this crime.

Romanovo-Borisoglebsk (now called Tutaev), though never a large place, boasts an enormous cathedral of the Yaroslavl type, but with two-storeyed galleries approached from the porches by covered flights of steps [Plate 44, 1].

At Rostov Veliki is a very remarkable assemblage of churches, for the most part built against the massive wall of the Kremlin itself, and flanked by defensive towers (plan, F, p. 42). The churches are two-storeyed, and in consequence unusually high, even in this country of tall churches [Plate 45]. The town, though of very ancient foundation, rose to greatest importance since the end of the sixteenth century, when it became the seat of a Metropolitan. It was during the episcopacy of a certain Jonas Sisoevich, and through his initiative, that were built most of the churches of Rostov, as well as those at Romanovo and Uglich.

Interesting monuments remain also in several little northern towns now reduced to an insignificance which makes the abundance of their churches astonishing. Such are Solikamsk on the Kama in the far east of European Russia, and Solvychegodsk on the Vychegda river, both owing their former prosperity to salt mines. Not far from Solvychegodsk, on the second of the sister streams which join together as the Northern Dvina, lies Veliki Ustyug, with its forest of churches. One of these, dedicated to the Ascension, and dating from 1648, has exceedingly rich and varied decoration in brick and plaster, showing a baroque tendency [Plate 46]. Excepting the great baroque church of Solvychegodsk, this is the most elaborate building in all northern Russia.

The subject of belfries and other towers is so large and important that it deserves a special mention. Since the sixteenth century, when "tent" belfries began to be used, they became immensely popular (especially after the proscription of "tents" on the churches themselves), and underwent something of an evolution on their own. At least, a sequence in type is clearly seen, though probably their development in time was not so well defined. The simplest form of conical tower, reminding one of the wooden "tent" churches themselves, has no openings and cannot, of course, be used for bells. There are examples at Sergievo, Yaroslavl, etc. [Plates 34, 3; 52, 1]. Of bell towers proper, the form most closely resembling their wooden prototype is that with a plain conical roof surmounting the arcaded storey where the bells are hung [Plate 52, 3]. From this evolves a type, unrepresented in wood, in which the roof is pierced by windows, either in a single tier, or in several. A beautiful tower in the Arbat at Moscow, now unfortunately pulled down, had no less than four such tiers of windows [Plates 35; 44, 3; 52; 53, etc.].

Other varieties of bell tower have abandoned the strict conical form. A type used at Yaroslavl and elsewhere rises in several storeys of diminishing diameter [Plate 54, 3, 4]. There are others of somewhat anomalous form, such as one at Pskov, and that of the Assumption in Pechatniki at Moscow [Plate 54, 1, 2]. The great bell tower of Ivan Veliki at Moscow represents another independent variety seldom repeated: it is rather imposing than beautiful in itself, as it soars above the many churches and palaces of the Kremlin [Plates 51; 64, 1]. Yet another form of tower is due to the Tartars, for it originates with the "Sumbeka Tower" of Kazan, built under the Tartar régime in the sixteenth century [Plate 55, 3]. The Borovitski tower on the Kremlin wall [Plate 55, 4] is a reproduction of it, and the modern building of the Kazan railway station at Moscow was based on the same model.

8. WOODEN ARCHITECTURE IN THE UKRAINE AND UKRAINIAN BAROQUE

In south-western Russia there exists a style of wooden architecture entirely distinct from that of the north. It is also less interesting in so far as it seems not to be an original creation of the Russians, but to be closely related to the wooden architecture of the eastern Carpathian region. Strzygowski, however, has drawn fresh attention to the style by his claim that it represents, in its three and fivefold plans, and in the construction of its cupolas, the most primitive architecture of the Aryan races as a whole, which style he traces from Kashmir westwards to every part of Europe.

Whatever the truth in Strzygowski's theories, it is at least established that the wooden architecture of the Ukraine has a long history, and that the surviving churches, late though they be, are the descendants of primitive wooden buildings of the pre-Christian period. It is usual to ascribe most of the details of the present churches to baroque influence coming in from Poland in the seventeenth century, when that country was very strongly imbued with the baroque spirit in architecture. But

the plans certainly show no such influence, and are probably retained
in a very primitive form.

There are two common types of church. One consists of three divisions in a straight line which, as in the northern wooden architecture,
represent vestibule, body of church, and sanctuary. The other type has
two additional elements to north and south, so that the plan, as a whole,
presents the form of a Greek cross (E, p. 65). In either case each division rises into a cupola [Plate 56]. But the Ukrainian type, with five
cupolas, bears no resemblance to the Russian five-domed church: the
former has its four extra domes on the axes of the church, the latter on
the diagonals. There exists also a simpler type, with but a single cupola,
and a more complex, with no less than nine, the building consisting
virtually of three churches side by side. The latter is very uncommon
and relatively modern, being represented in the Ukraine only by a very
few examples.

The system of construction in all these churches is the same as that
used in north Russia, and characteristic, in fact, of the Slavs generally
—that is, by the piling up of horizontal timbers interlocking at the
corners. (Strzygowski's "block-work" in contradistinction to the
"frame-work" of western Europe.) Roofs are either raftered, or else
continue the "block-work" of the walls, taking, in that case, the form
of cupolas. In these the transition from square to octagon is effected by
means of beams placed across the corners of the square, a system to
which Strzygowski attaches great importance, as being the original
Aryan principle of construction, which influenced the development of
brick and stone vaulting in northern Iran. More will be heard of this
subject in the account of Transcaucasian architecture.[1]

Comparison of the various Ukrainian churches leads to the conclusion, however, that their primitive covering was no form of cupola, but
a raftered roof having the form of a blunt pyramid. Such roofs must
necessarily spring from a square base, and there can be no doubt that
the early churches, like most of the recent ones, were built up of simple

[1] P. 77.

rectangular units. About the details of these vanished buildings nothing can be said. Almost all the existing ones (of which none is older than the seventeenth century) show strong baroque influence. This is seen in the use of polygonal instead of square elements, the breaking up of plain walls into facets, and the great heightening and elaboration of cupolas. These cupolas, and, in fact, the whole church, were generally divided into several storeys, most commonly a square base supporting octagons each smaller than the one below. The successive storeys are often separated by slanting roofs, and these may be prolonged into enormous eaves, giving a strikingly pagoda-like aspect to the building [Plate 56, 4].

The style known as Ukrainian baroque, the counterpart in brick of the wooden architecture just described, owes its being to the same penetration of baroque details from Poland, that had so strong an influence on the wooden style. It is absurd to state, as at least one writer has done, that Ukrainian wooden building is simply a reflection in another material of the Ukrainian baroque. Both styles were simultaneously affected by the western influence, but of the two, it was the wooden style that showed greater strength and independence, and did itself, to some extent, influence Ukrainian baroque—as it influenced also, and very markedly, the baroque of Moscow.

Baroque architecture in the Ukraine did not produce a single building of outstanding beauty or interest. Indeed, it was scarcely an independent style, for it showed itself most often as an unpleasant incrustation on the ancient Byzantine buildings of Kiev and other cities [Plate 57]. Credit is due, however, to some of the architects of this period for preserving, by their restorations, several ancient churches which would otherwise have disappeared. Such new buildings as they did erect either followed the Russian five-domed tradition, or were given the basilican plan of catholic churches in Poland. Their details differ in no way from those of the baroque style elsewhere in Europe. The walls are laden with twisted pilasters, elaborate window frames, broken and distorted pediments,[1] etc., and the cupolas take on complex and fantastic outlines.

From the general point of view of Russian architectural history, the interest of these two styles, Ukrainian wood and Ukrainian baroque, lies in their effect on the development of architecture in Moscow. The former style contributed new suggestions in the matter of general form and plan; the latter handed on its heritage of baroque ornament. The result was the appearance, in Moscow, of a style much more pleasing and interesting than the Ukrainian baroque by whose agency it came into being.

9. BAROQUE OF MOSCOW

More circumstances than one had laid Muscovy open to Western influence since the sixteenth century. From being a completely isolated and land-locked country, Muscovy had been drawn into the general orbit of European inter-relationships. The Archangel route provided an open road to western Europe, and the absorption of the Tartar Khanates in the south had freed Russia's natural southern outlet through the Black Sea and the Mediterranean. At the same time, every foreign power of importance had its Embassy in Moscow, and travellers and traders began to come in ever increasing numbers. At Yaroslavl there were French, Dutch, English, and Spaniards.

In Moscow itself, since the time of Boris Godunov (end of sixteenth century), there had been a considerable foreign population. Many of these foreigners were traders; others were mercenaries employed by the Tsars in an effort to build up an efficient army on west European lines, or experts in the manufacture of weapons and ammunition. Not all the Russians, however, appreciated these foreigners. The Church especially

---

[1] Originally the triangular space enclosed between the top of a portico and the two sides of the roof above. The word is applied to any ornamental feature of the same general shape over a door or window. In the baroque style pediments may assume very various forms, some utterly fantastic.

saw with much disfavour the presence in their midst of a large heretical population, and Russian traders resented the competition of rivals more capable than themselves. As an outcome of pressure from these sources, an Imperial decree was issued in 1652 requiring all foreigners to live in a special suburb of Moscow, the *Nemetskaya Sloboda*,[1] and forbidding them to mix with the general population. The result, as it turned out, was precisely the opposite of that intended. The influence of the foreigners, now concentrated together, became stronger than ever. It was here that Peter the Great's father, and Peter himself, were introduced to the customs of western Europe. The *Nemetskaya Sloboda* became, indeed, the real centre of westernisation in Russia.

An event still more significant in the westernisation of Russian art (though politically of less consequence) was the annexation of the Ukraine in 1654. This was the outcome, not of armed conquest, but of a friendly treaty between the two countries—Great Russia and Little Russia. Little Russia (or the Ukraine) did not then cover the same area as it now does. The right bank of the Dnieper, excluding a small area around Kiev, remained, at this time, a part of Poland. Through its close connection with Poland, Little Russia was strongly imbued with Latin culture, and, as has been seen, with the baroque taste in architecture.

After its annexation by Muscovite Russia, the way was open for the assimilation by Moscow of the baroque style, a process encouraged by the already active westernisation which had been gathering force, from the causes mentioned above, throughout the seventeenth century. It was not, however, until the last twenty years of the century that Muscovite architecture assumed full right to be described as baroque. There are many churches in this style clustering about Moscow, and within the city itself; further afield, it did not meet with wide popularity.

Some baroque churches keep to the traditional square plan, and the central cupola is surrounded by four others on the corners. An example is St Nicholas "of the Great Cross" in Moscow, with its elaborate columns and capitals, contorted pediments, Italian shells, and domes

---

[1] Literally the "German Liberty".

encrusted with golden stars [Plate 58, 1]. More often, however, they follow one or other of the forms suggested by Ukrainian wooden architecture. The little church of the "Vladimir Mother of God" in the Kitai Gorod repeats a single-domed type from the Ukraine; its spiky dome recalls one of those of St Basil [Plate 61, 1]. The Novodevichi Monastery has a number of excellent examples of the style. Among them the Church of the Intercession takes after the Ukrainian three-domed plan, and several towers show the "storeyed" arrangement originating in the same region [Plate 60].

The storeyed church is often combined with the Ukrainian five-domed cruciform plan. The result is seen in the peculiar church at Fili near Moscow. It is further distinguished by the four massive stairways which lead to an open gallery surrounding its base [Plate 59, 1]. A glance at the plans on p. 65 (E, F) at once makes apparent the relationship between this building and Ukrainian wooden churches. A still stranger church is that of Dubrovitski, which, like Fili, was the whim of a wealthy landowner. It too has a four-lobed plan, and from its centre rises a great tower thickly plastered with luxuriant baroque ornament.

The Church of the Assumption in the district of Pokrovka, which excited Napoleon's approval, is decidedly original. Along its main east-west axis the three principal domes are arranged, as well as a bell tower; but to north and south of the central mass, which rises in three stages, is a pair of subsidiary domes on either side [Plate 58, 2].

Outside Moscow, the five-domed plan with cruciform (Ukrainian) arrangement recurs at Nizhni Novgorod, in a church completed about 1719 [Plate 61, 4]. Among other provincial examples the most elaborate is one at Solvychegodsk in the north, dating from the end of the seventeenth century. It follows the old Russian five-domed plan, and, like the church of Nizhni, is covered with typical baroque detail in immense profusion. Both these elaborate buildings are due to the munificence of the Stroganovs, a great trading family in mediaeval Russia.

Towers of the period are seldom tent-shaped, but rise in a number of stories; a fine specimen is the great belfry of the Novodevichi Monastery

[Plate 60, 3]. The Sukharev tower, one of Moscow's most conspicuous landmarks, built in his youth by Peter the Great, has a gigantic rectangular base from which rises a comparatively graceful belfry-like tower of the old tent-roofed form [Plate 59, 2]. The style is thoroughly baroque, much resembling that of the church at Fili.

These form, on the whole, an original and a pleasing group of monuments. The career of the style would no doubt have been a longer one, but it was cut short abruptly in 1714, when Peter the Great promulgated his *ukaz*, prohibiting all building, except in wood, anywhere outside his new capital, St Petersburg. That was almost the final blow to the native architecture of Russia. Thereafter, as part of the policy of forcible modernisation pursued by Peter the Great, a species of classicism was introduced, which, of whatever interest on its own account—and some have found it worthy of study—owed absolutely nothing to the Russian tradition in architecture.

Succeeding generations saw, indeed, some continuance of the Russo-baroque style into the eighteenth and nineteenth centuries. To Rastrelli, one of the many Italians who have taken their part in Russian architectural history, are due not only various palaces of Petersburg and Tsarskoe Selo, but not a few religious buildings scattered about the country. One may mention the bell towers of the great monasteries at Kiev and Sergievo [Plate 65, 1]. The Smolny Monastery at Petersburg would indeed have made an imposing pile if the projected bell tower had ever been built.

There is little else to command one's admiration. Most later baroque creations show a preference for the cruciform five-domed arrangement, or, especially in humbler churches, for the single dome. Often their towers, with a tapering *flèche* derived from western Europe, are the most pleasing feature of the composition [Plate 62].

In modern times there has been attempted the resuscitation of the old Russian style, and its products are seen in such distressing buildings as the Historical Museum in Moscow. This "revival" resulted, in fact, as has often happened in like cases elsewhere, in rather dismal failure.

10. WOODEN ARCHITECTURE OF THE SEVENTEENTH AND EIGHTEENTH CENTURIES

It may seem unjustifiable to include in a description of "mediaeval" architecture, not merely buildings of late date reproducing ancient forms, but also entirely new types developed no earlier than the latter part of the seventeenth and the beginning of the eighteenth century. Yet Russia at this time was still mediaeval in almost every sense, and, in spite of Peter the Great's tremendous changes in the towns, rural Russia, and more especially the north, remained in a mediaeval stage of civilisation throughout the eighteenth century, if not beyond it.

One character of the northern architecture itself gives the period in question a distinctively mediaeval stamp, shared with the great building epochs of western Europe. The architecture appears to have undergone a spontaneous evolution, in which the builders themselves were passive participants. There were, indeed, individual builders of genius, but their ideal was not so much a personal as a national one, and they were free from the self-consciousness of modern architects. They never consciously returned to old models for inspiration; they certainly based their work on what came immediately before, but never slavishly copied it; they made additions and improvements of their own. The church-building carpenters of the north were associated in itinerant guilds (*artel*), and were employed by villages requiring a new church. The contracts drawn up often included an elaborate specification of the church to be built. This ensured the active participation of the villagers themselves, who had very definite tastes, in the development of their own archi-tecture. It may therefore be said that the wooden architecture of north Russia is a direct expression of the national taste and the national genius. As in mediaeval Europe, style succeeded style in time, while different areas developed their own favourite forms. But, owing to the exceptional difficulty of communications in northern Russia, there was less uniformity of style over the whole area. Now, when even the latest monuments of the style are terribly decimated by fire, their distribution seems even more patchy and erratic.

One historical event proved very favourable to the development of wooden architecture. This was the schism, within the Orthodox Russian Church, between the supporters of the Patriarch Nikon, whose "reforms" involved a return to primitive Greek ritual, and the dissenting "Old Believers" who refused to give up the procedure long established in Russia. The dissenters (*raskólnik*) were expelled from the Church and ruthlessly persecuted. They fled from Moscow and took refuge in obscure parts of the country, but especially in the far north, where they continued to build wooden churches and worship in their own way. Often they suffered martyrdom by fire within the walls of their own churches. For two hundred and fifty years—from the middle of the seventeenth century until the enforced reforms of 1905—the Old Believers continued to be persecuted by Church and State. The work of their hands remains in many admirable old churches round the White Sea and on the banks of the northern rivers.

Earlier in this outline were mentioned those types of wooden church which existed almost certainly in the sixteenth century, and were thus enabled to influence very considerably the history of brick architecture in Moscow. Besides the oldest and simplest types of rectangular and octagonal churches, it appeared that the cruciform variety with super-posed *bochki* had already come into existence. Other of the more complex types may also have been developed at the same time, but it is more convenient to refer to them all here, and it was certainly during the later period now being considered that these elaborated forms experienced their greatest expansion and met with widest popularity.

One notices at once that the most characteristic type of the first half of the seventeenth century has now disappeared—I refer to the "tented" church on octagonal plan, with simple projections to east and west. The explanation is perhaps to be found in the Church edict of 1650, which insisted on the square Byzantine plan. It required also the abandonment of the tent roof, but this, at first, was more than the northern builders could tolerate, and tented churches continued to be built well into the eighteenth century. In the north, remote from the interference of Church and State, it was possible to ignore for a time their requirements in church building, and at a later stage, when the letter of the edict appeared to be fulfilled, a very near approach to the favourite "tented" church was still achieved.

The adoption of a square plan for tented churches involved practically the combination of two types, the rectangular and the octagonal, for the "tent" roof had been a direct development from, and an intrinsic part of the octagonal plan. The central square was now made to pass up into an octagon, the transition being achieved by cross-beams cutting off the corners, and the octagon was still crowned by a tapering conical roof. The church at Kondopoga on Lake Onega is a very late example of this kind. It is singularly tall and narrow, and, with the unusual arrangement of its stairways, offers a most charming silhouette. In all churches of this type, the eastern projection, which contains the altar, is short and tall; the western one, on the other hand, is relatively low and long. The result is a very beautiful balance in the proportions [Plates 70, 71].

A development from this type, in which several elements having the form above described are combined in a single building, occurs round the shores of the White Sea (plan, C, p. 65). A very attractive example is the old cathedral of Kem on the western coast. It is one of the very few specimens of wooden architecture to be seen in the towns of northern Russia; almost all are buried in remote and inaccessible villages. The church of Kem is triple, for the larger central element is flanked by two similar, but smaller ones. Unfortunately, in common with very many such churches, it has been covered with commonplace boarding which obscures the round interlocking logs of the original, and other damage was done in the course of a restoration [Plate 72]. At Nyónoksa, between Onega and Archangel, is a similar structure with no less than four tents, of which two rise from the central division of the building.

The cruciform church shows innumerable varieties. In these the central square has projections on all four sides, not to east and west only. It has been suggested that the extra extensions were added in an effort to obscure the rectangular lines of the square with which the builders were loth to replace their favourite octagon. The result, in any case, was a church cruciform in plan. In the simplest case the arms of the cross were crowned with single *bochki* applied to the walls of the central square. The latter often finished in the traditional tent roof; sometimes in a group of cupolas [Plate 73, 1]. A further development is seen in the use of *bochki* in two tiers, as at Varzuga, on the northern, and Una on the southern coast of the White Sea [Plate 73, 2]. Some of these churches are prodigiously tall, the central element being prolonged upwards like a tower, and the four projections, falling into insignificance, are closely applied to its walls. There are many such along the course of the Northern Dvina. Others are more spread out, so that the central unit loses its pre-eminence to the advantage of the arms of the cross.

A peculiar class of church is very common in the region of Onega, but rare elsewhere. It is described as "alembic-roofed" or "ark-roofed", but neither term is particularly descriptive. The central square in these churches is surmounted by a roof which has, in vertical section (or in silhouette), the form of a bulbous dome or *bochka*. The origin of this peculiar roof is quite unknown; perhaps it was an entirely original creation. It may carry a single dome, or five, conventionally disposed, or even more, in various arrangements. In many cases, however, as in both churches of Podporozhie, near Onega, other domes, independent of the principal roof, are so arranged that they lead up to the central cluster; the whole building then acquires that conical outline after which the northern architects constantly strove. These churches either show three divisions along the east-west axis, or are cruciform; both plans occur at Podporozhie [Plate 74].

There exist in the north a few wooden churches which are clearly copied directly from the standard five-domed plan usual in brick architecture. But the northern architects generally showed more originality, however great the influence of brick (and it was necessarily considerable) at this period. Thus a form with nine cupolas, resting either on a square or an octagon, exists on Lake Onega, and was once plentiful in the neighbourhood of Archangel. It was apparently derived from the form with five cupolas by inserting an extra one in the middle of each side. At Kizhi, however, this primitive arrangement is lost; the central square is converted into an octagon, whose corners bear the eight outer cupolas in a circle [Plate 75, 1].

One more fundamental form of wooden church remains. This is the "storeyed" church, roughly resembling those of the Ukraine. These are built up of successive octagons, or else, as at Kandalaksha on the Arctic coast of the White Sea, of octagons alternating with squares. It may be that this type was actually imported from the Ukraine, for an Ukrainian immigration to the north took place in the seventeenth century [Plate 75, 2].

In the course of the eighteenth century these numerous types of church were combined in various ways to produce an almost infinite variety of form and proportion. A common practice of the later period was the combination, almost for the first time, of church and bell tower, a process the earlier builders had rarely attempted. An example is the second wooden church at Kem on the White Sea, though this one gives an impression of degeneration in its squat proportions [Plate 79]. A small and pleasing specimen I found isolated in the fields a few miles from Kizhi; but they occur almost anywhere [Plate 78]. Separate bell towers remain as common as ever. In this period they are provided always with a square base, which shows a tendency to become more prominent in later towers. In the eighteenth century, the conical roof is sometimes replaced by a flattish dome bearing a spike or *flèche* [Plate 81].

Among the many and various creations of this very live style of the eighteenth century, the most remarkable of all, without question, is the astonishing church at Kizhi, which stands on an island in Lake Onega

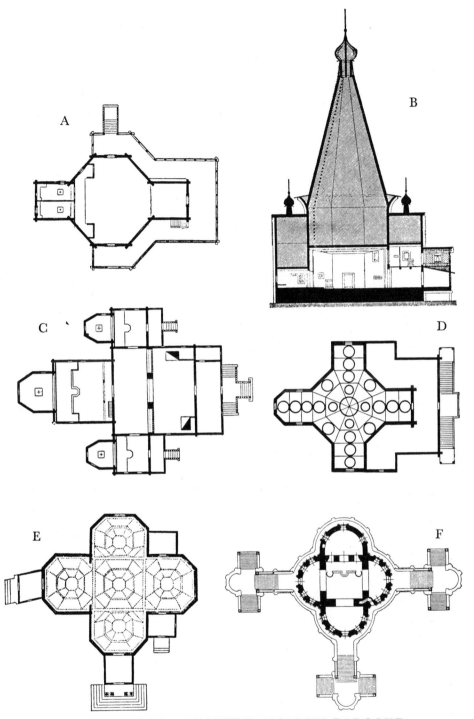

WOODEN ARCHITECTURE, MOSCOW BAROQUE

NORTHERN WOOD: A. Plan of octagonal tent-roofed church at Belaya Sluda.
B. Longitudinal section of the same church showing the confined internal space.
C. Plan of rectangular tent-roofed church at Kem. D. Church at Kizhi. Plan
showing positions of the twenty-two domes.

UKRAINIAN WOOD: E. Plan of typical five-domed cruciform church.

MOSCOW BAROQUE: F. Plan of the church at Fili, near Moscow, showing relationship to Ukrainian wooden architecture.

[Plates 76, 77]. Truly this is a work of genius, however wild and fantastic an outburst of the national taste in architecture. It is, perhaps, as great an oddity in the world of wood as is St Basil in the world of brick; but in neither is there anything absolutely new, no detail or system that cannot definitely be traced back to a line of prototypes.

The church of Kizhi is octagonal in plan, but from alternate sides of the octagon there project short extensions forming the arms of a cross (plan D, p. 65). Above each of these arms is built up a series of no less than four (at the east end five) *bochki*, each carrying a bulbous dome which, by virtue of its similar form, fits neatly into the *bochka* above. At the level of the third tier, the intermediate sides of the building likewise have each their *bochka* and dome. The four flights of domes lead one's eye upward to the topmost and twenty-second, which crowns the whole. But this is simply the peak of a complex pile in which no one part is specially emphasised at the expense of another. On the western side of the church is a huge double stairway or *kryltso* [Plate 77, 2]. Each flight of stairs is approached through a small porch with double-sloping roof, and at the top is a wide common platform, giving access to the narthex or *trapeznaya*. The church itself is resplendent inside with icons and gilded ornament, but gives no suggestion of its astounding outward form.

This great pyramid of domes makes indeed a striking landmark, raising high its pointed form among the maze of low-lying islands scattered in the vast expanse of Lake Onega. It is a remote and lonely place that enshrines this masterpiece of the old Russian church builders. But one may truly say that nowhere in the country, not in Moscow, not in Yaroslavl or any of the great Volga towns, can a church be found so fully expressing the Russian genius in architecture, and according so genuinely with the people's taste.

PART II
TRANSCAUCASIA

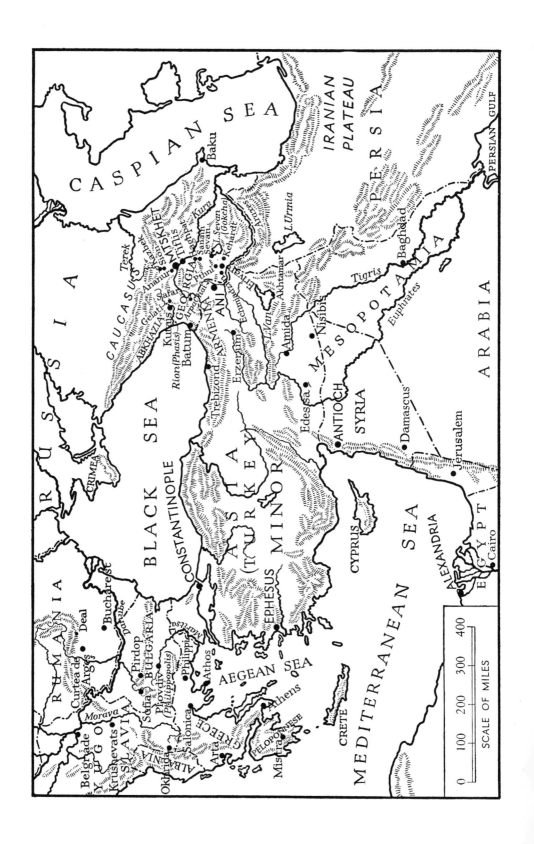

INTRODUCTORY

THE architecture of Transcaucasia has but little in common with that of Russia. In fact, in almost all respects, the two styles show marked contrasts, and their relationship is probably remote and indirect. As to what exactly that relationship is, opinions differ widely with the various schools of thought. The most conservative school would make them cousins with a common ancestry in Constantinople, while Strzygowski's highly unorthodox theories make the style of Armenia the parent stock from which sprang the Byzantine of Constantinople as well as the Byzantine of Kiev.

Apart from this question of genetic relationship between the two styles, there arises another: to what extent was Russian architecture, especially of the Vladimir period, subject to influence from beyond the Caucasus? References have been made in the Russian section to this interesting problem, which provides one excuse for the inclusion here of a description of Transcaucasian architecture. The other reason for this conjunction is that both styles are found within the territory of the Soviet Union in Europe, and modern geography connects them closely, even though the ancient barrier of the great Caucasian range long kept them rigidly apart.

Whatever differences of opinion remain—and they are neither few nor insignificant—one fact emerges from recent study of Caucasian architecture: that it was not a mere provincial style of the Byzantine Empire, as is still irresponsibly stated. Strzygowski, at the other extreme, makes it not only independent of Byzantium but the immediate inspirer of Byzantine architecture itself. Not only so, he would derive largely from Armenian sources the Romanesque of Italy, Spain, France, Germany and Britain, even the new forms of the Italian Renaissance. Strzygowski allows little to Greece, nothing to Rome. His greatest antagonist is Rivoira, who ascribes to the initiative of his countrymen, and especially to Rome, the whole credit for architectural progress at home and a large share in the origin of Byzantine; and derives directly from Lombard architecture all those styles which flourished north of the Alps from the tenth century onwards. Between these points of view there lies no doubt a compromise containing a greater measure of truth than either extreme.

In any case the study of Transcaucasian architecture is far more complex than that of Russian, which can conveniently be followed almost in isolation. The history of architecture in any country of western Asia is intimately bound up with that of every other style in this great region. The subject of Transcaucasia is, indeed, so large and complex, and beset with so many difficulties and differences of opinion, that it cannot here be explored in detail. I shall first mention the most conspicuous of the general characteristics of the style, and give in what follows a brief account of its supposed origin and lines of evolution.

The styles I have referred to as Transcaucasian are in reality two: Armenian and Georgian. They are commonly spoken of together as Armenian, but this is hardly justified. The Armenians were apparently the originators of both styles,[1] and from the beginning to about the tenth century were the principal builders, whether what they built stands now within the borders of Armenia, or in Georgia, or in other countries whose people took no part in architectural history. Since the time, however, when Georgia gained the upper hand in Transcaucasia, and especially during the brilliant period of her civilisation under the Bagratids from the eleventh to the thirteenth century, the main initiative in building was with the Georgians, and in their hands the style underwent some change which entitles it to rank as distinct from that of Armenia. During this later period much of the same country was again covered with churches, but their centre of distribution was more northerly, and the majority of buildings in the Georgian style are found within the modern boundaries of that country.

[1] Chubinashvili would claim a great degree of independence for Georgia.

The history of this architecture practically ceases in the thirteenth century, for though Georgia retained her independence long after the fall and dismemberment of Armenia—right on, indeed, until the advent of the Russians at the beginning of the nineteenth century—her history was a perpetual struggle against aggression from all sides, and neither time nor wealth nor energy were left for the pursuit of art.

Since the thirteenth century, there has been virtually no evolution in the Transcaucasian styles. A few churches were built in the course of centuries and many have appeared in recent times, especially in Tiflis, the modern capital of Transcaucasia; but they show no originality beyond a tendency to heightening and attenuation, so common in the later history of other styles.

In general appearance the churches of Transcaucasus are far more uniformly pleasing than those of Russia. One feels that the Caucasian architects regularly reached a plane of conception and achievement to which the Russians rose but seldom. In styles so different, however, such comparisons have little value. In any case, other circumstances than the gifts of the architects contributed to this result. In the Caucasian region there was available a variety of building stones equalled, in the Byzantine world, only in parts of Syria and Asia Minor. Therefore, the building material invariably used was stone. Usually the walls were built of a very hard rubble concrete beautifully faced with stone. As with the stone churches of Vladimir, this invited carving, and stone carving, often extremely beautiful and elaborate, is a constant character in all churches from about the tenth century onward. It is used both inside and out, and almost displaces the coloured surface decoration—fresco and mosaic—found in all brick churches of the true Byzantine and Russian styles.

The later, and by far the most widespread type of church in Armenia and Georgia shows a certain uniformity in outward form. It presents the appearance of a basilica, in which the slope of the roof is broken, and across the centre of which is placed a short transept, usually not extending beyond the basilican walls. All the roofs are straight and gabled, showing no outward trace of vaulting. Over the crossing is placed a single cupola, whose dome takes the outward form of a cone, though a true hemisphere within. This conical dome is as characteristic of Armenian and Georgian architecture as is the bulb of Russian; it is universal except in some of the earliest buildings.

The straight lines of roofs and dome, which mark off the styles of Transcaucasus so conspicuously from all other forms of Byzantine architecture, are a natural consequence of building in stone to the exclusion of all other materials. Both roof and domes were always covered with stone slabs, and it would obviously be difficult to make such a facing conform to curved outlines following the form of the vaults.

Some, especially Georgian churches, show a rather striking resemblance to contemporary Romanesque structures in western Europe. They show the same material, the same round arches, recessed doorways, and blind arcades, and many striking similarities in the sculptured ornament. Baltrušaitis, who has recently studied the subject in minute detail, finds, however, a fundamental divergence in the relationship of ornamentation to the general mass. In the Romanesque churches ornament is subsidiary to structure, is used in conjunction with structure, and serves to emphasise it. In Transcaucasia, on the contrary, ornament is independent, and serves rather to mask the structure of the building than to express it.

The Armenians and Georgians have been criticised as builders, and in truth one could not claim that they reached the standards of mediaeval architects in western Europe. Yet the survival of many of their churches for a thousand years and more, after centuries of neglect, and in spite of the earthquakes prevailing in that unstable part of the earth's surface, is a high tribute to those who built them. Certainly, a majority of these churches are small. In a wholly mountainous country there cannot be the same incentive to building on a really large scale; conversely, one may remember that all the great cathedrals of western Europe are placed in the flattest districts. The efforts of Armenian and

Georgian architects were never directed towards a great increase in the size of their churches.

One tendency of the Caucasian builders is so marked as almost to constitute a character of the style. They made every effort to perch their churches in as conspicuous a place as possible, often on top of a hill, even on the face of a cliff—a custom going far to make up for their small dimensions. This practice must often have involved the greatest difficulties in building; but it gives in return an extraordinary picturesqueness to many a Caucasian landscape.

Scheme of design from the church of Tsminda Sameba
near Kazbek, Georgia.

HISTORICAL OUTLINE

1. ORIGINS

THE origin of Armenian architecture is a subject of much heated controversy between the rival schools of Rivoira and Strzygowski. To the latter, however, is due the credit of having for the first time made an exhaustive study of the Armenian style, the results of his researches being embodied in the two huge volumes of *Die Baukunst der Armenier und Europa*. Rivoira's not entirely convincing arguments on the other side appeared in his *Moslem Architecture*, but this was originally published before Strzygowski's principal work.

Armenia was certainly in a position to receive influences either from the West or the East. Throughout its history the country has been a bone of contention between eastern and western powers. About the second century B.C. Armenia was influenced by Greek culture, but was never "hellenised" as were Asia Minor and Syria. Later, during the first centuries B.C. and A.D. the country became a petty protectorate of Rome. In the third century Christianity came to Armenia from Cappadocia in eastern Asia Minor, and it was at Caesarea in that country that Gregory "The Illuminator", the apostle of Armenia, received his training. In the fourth century there was still opportunity for Roman influence: Armenia was partitioned between Rome and Persia. It was not until the end of the fifth century that Armenia's ecclesiastical dependence on Constantinople came to an end.

Thus historical facts do not necessarily run counter to Rivoira's belief that Armenian architecture had its origin, along with all the architectures of Europe, in Rome and Ravenna. He finds Roman plans from which those of Armenia could have been developed. He sees in the blind arcades and the elaborate sculpture of Armenian exteriors ideas imported directly from the architecture of the Lombards. Even the squinch[1] and the pendentive[2] are derived from Rome and denied to Armenia or any Eastern country, for "the vital discoveries of vaulted architecture were essentially the legacy of the West".

Strzygowski sees in Rivoira's theories the combined operation of local patriotism and the force of tradition, and it is true that until the end of the last century no theories existed that did not derive all western and middle eastern architecture from Greece and Rome exclusively. Strzygowski himself was the first to draw attention to the importance of the East in the origin and development of many important architectural forms. An attempt will now be made to summarise his theories in so far as they affect the history of architecture in Armenia.

During the first three centuries of the Christian era there occurred an immense expansion of Christianity in the East. It found first a fertile soil in the great Hellenistic cities of the Mediterranean, but extended thereafter, in the hands of Nestorian missionaries, far beyond through Persia and central Asia, eventually as far as Chinese Turkestan and China itself. Tiridates of Armenia accepted Christianity as his State religion (as much, it is true, as a political weapon against the Zoroastrian Persians, as for its own sake), even before the new faith was tolerated by Rome. In other of these countries it would have become as firmly established as in Europe but for the rise and spread of younger religions. Thus the Mediterranean region was not the only focus of Christian civilisation. The cities of northern Mesopotamia, Edessa (Urfa), Nisibin (Nisibis) and, somewhat later, Amida (Diyarbekr), were a great cultural and missionary centre in "Hither Asia" towards which, rather than towards the Mediterranean, looked Asia Minor and Syria. The importance of this whole region in architectural as in general history has been sadly neglected in the past. Yet the peoples of nearer Asia created at this early period a Christian art and architecture of their own, which had no small influence in the West.

In his earlier books Strzygowski set out to combat the accepted theory

[1] See p. 77.   [2] See note, p. 13.

that all Christian art emanated from Rome; he proposed instead a major share in this process to the countries of the eastern Mediterranean—to Egypt, to Syria, and to Asia Minor. In these countries there were local traditions of building, traditions of eastern origin, and these became fused with a Greek element introduced through their respective coastal cities—Alexandria, Antioch, and Ephesus. The result in each country was a compound style of peculiar vigour, owing absolutely nothing to Rome, and from these sources Strzygowski derived the principal inspiration in the early development of Christian art.

But his point of view has changed. Having demolished Rome, he set to work to do the same for Greece and the Eastern Empire. In successive works he progressively reduced the importance of the Hellenistic element, and finally denied it even the smallest share in the origin of Christian art, whether of architecture or ornament; Constantinople, Ephesus, Antioch, Alexandria, count for nothing. He now finds the origin of all things in central and western Asia; more precisely, in Aryan Persia and Semitic Mesopotamia.

In the first few centuries A.D. the Church had as yet adopted no particular style of architecture, and local Christian communities freely built in whatever style they found in use on the spot. Thus there was nothing to prevent the assimilation of Asiatic ideas into Christian architecture, and their transmission westwards to Europe. There can no longer be much serious doubt that this in fact occurred. But whereas Strzygowski now claims Armenia to have been the only intermediary of importance in the westward transmission of Asiatic forms, most other authorities would allow a share to Syria (especially in ornament) and Asia Minor (especially in architecture).

It has been assumed in the past, and is still reasonably maintained by some, that in the origin of her own architecture Armenia owes much to these same regions. They were not, however, the only countries from which it was possible for Armenia to draw architectural inspiration. To the east lay the great Iranian plateau, including all the modern Persia together with Afghanistan and Baluchistan. It is in northern Iran, with its Aryan population, that Strzygowski sees the real place of origin of Armenian architecture. The fundamental unit of the style is the dome raised over a square bay, and it is this basic element which originates, apparently, in the desert plateau of central Asia.

Pursuing his principle of the wooden derivation of all important styles, and assuming, probably with justification, the former existence of great tracts of forests in parts of western and central Asia, he postulates a wooden archetype of the domed square. He asserts that such a structure was characteristic of the primitive architecture of the Aryan peoples as a whole, and deduces its actual form from modern representatives of the type, notably from recent wooden dwelling houses in the Himalayan region, and from some forms of wooden church in the Ukraine (south-west Russia). These both show a method of covering the square by means of horizontal pieces laid successively across the corners, the process being continued until the space is roofed in.

Such a method of construction is supposed to have been copied in sun-dried brick by the people of northern Iran, when and where timber was not available. To represent the wooden corner-pieces in their very different material, the builders in brick placed little arches across the corners of the square, and from the round or polygonal base so formed a dome was raised. In parts of Persia dwelling huts are built to this day on the same principle; and in the dry climate of central Asia just such villages have been preserved from very remote times.

The same plan, with dome superimposed on the square, was now translated by the Armenians into their particular materials, which were stone and rubble. The brick corner arches of the Iranians became the stone "squinch", which (contrary to Rivoira's assertion) was the first method by which the Armenians raised their domes over a square [Plate 89, 3].

As Strzygowski says, an architectural form has little chance of development so long as it is used exclusively for private domestic purposes. Thus it was the Armenians who, with their demand for halls of assembly and places of Christian worship, first built the domed square on a really monumental scale, and in their masterly hands it developed into the innumerable varieties of church which appeared in Transcaucasia between the sixth and thirteenth centuries.

In Asia itself Strzygowski finds also the home of those systems of geometrical ornament which the various peoples of that continent, including the Armenians, have used and elaborated. He distinguishes two racial sources from which came two fundamentally different ornamental systems, but both purely conventional, in strong contrast to the ornament of all peoples under Hellenistic or Semitic influence. Thus the nomadic Turko-Mongolian people of the Altai region were responsible for that type of conventional decoration founded on a twisting stem, which gives off leaf-like processes alternately to either side. On the other hand the Indo-Aryans of the Iranian Plateau originated the interlacing type of geometrical ornament, which in later times achieved such worldwide popularity. The Arabs adopted both systems as they came in contact with these peoples, and for a time used them independently; the first gave rise to the "arabesque", the second to that form of design composed of interlocking polygons which the Arabs developed to an extraordinary degree of complexity.

Another type of ornament altogether, complicating the tangled relationships of these middle eastern styles, is that which developed in the southern part of the west Asiatic province under the influence of Hellenistic "representational" or realistic art. A tendency to render animate forms with a realistic intention prevailed among the Semites (Aramaeans) of Mesopotamia, in southern Persia, and in Syria. Into this art were introduced many striking subjects, having their origin in the more ancient arts of Babylonia and Assyria; such are the winged beasts and centaurs, lions, warriors with bows and arrows, etc.— subjects which are all characteristic of south Persian art, especially of the Sassanian dynasty.

In due course all these forms of ornamental art made their appearance in Transcaucasia, whether derived directly from their sources, or through the mediation of the various peoples with whom the Armenians and Georgians came in contact in the course of their history.

Thus Strzygowski's hypothesis—a most revolutionary one when first propounded—derives Armenian architecture and, in all essentials, Armenian decoration, exclusively from the East; it attributes to the Armenians themselves the entire responsibility for the great variety of plans elaborated in that country; and it claims nothing less than the descent of all mediaeval architecture in the West from the Armenian style itself.

An attractive hypothesis, but one not free from weaknesses. It cannot be proved that the earliest architecture of the Armenians was an adaptation of the Iranian domed square; as a matter of fact the oldest buildings in that country are basilicas imported from Syria and Asia Minor. Still less can it be proved that from Armenia alone did this domed square spread to the other countries of western Asia and eastern Europe. Earlier examples of it actually exist in Syria and Asia Minor, and in Italy; its previous existence in Armenia is a matter of conjecture. Moreover, why should the Armenians have adopted an architectural form from those who were their enemies, political and religious, rather than from other neighbouring peoples with whom they had friendly relations and a religion in common? Macler and others attach great importance to the Syrian connection, and claim that the domed square itself originated there. There is no doubt that in the fifth century Syrian and Anatolian influence was strong in the country, and no buildings in Transcaucasia remain from an earlier date; in fact, the first domed churches are no earlier than the middle of the sixth. One is therefore obliged to keep an open mind on this complicated subject, and hope that future investigation will throw a clearer light upon it.

2. ARMENIA BEFORE THE TENTH CENTURY: EVOLUTION IN CHURCH PLANS

It is probable that the earliest buildings in Armenia were themselves wooden, and that this explains the absence of certainly dated remains before the sixth century. About that time, however, the first stone churches began to make their appearance on the soil of Transcaucasia.

During the sixth, seventh and eighth centuries two principal types of church existed side by side in the present territory of Armenia and Georgia. One type was the "centralised" church, consisting fundamentally of the dome over a square bay, and originally imported (in Strzygowski's view) from northern Iran. Already by the sixth century this had been accepted by the Armenians as the basis of their national style, and from this starting point was developed a whole host of derivatives. The other form of church which appears in Armenia at the same time, a form as far removed as possible from the "centralised", was the vaulted basilica. It was a foreign and intrusive type, not willingly accepted in Armenia, where it survived only a few centuries. Its appearance in the country at all was due to the efforts of certain Armenian bishops who, as a result of relations with the Christians of Syria and Mesopotamia, wished to introduce a type of church there considered orthodox. According to Strzygowski, the barrel vault, and the vaulted basilica which embodies it, originated in Mesopotamia, and spread thence to Armenia, Syria and Europe.

The Transcaucasian basilicas may have one nave, but usually there are three, and in one peculiar variety these are completely cut off from each other by continuous walls. The most usual type, however, has a double row of pillars dividing the space longitudinally into nave and aisles, each separately vaulted. In correspondence with this internal division, the slope of the roof is broken by a short vertical stretch located above the two rows of pillars. Examples of basilicas from the sixth or seventh centuries occur at Tiflis, and at Sion high up in the Caucasus [Plate 83, 2]. At Ereruk in Armenia is the ruin of one of the finest basilicas in the world; the architects seem to have expended their genius as liberally on that building as on the native domed churches which were their special province. After the eighth century the basilican plan becomes scarce.

In the centralised church the longitudinal axis is subordinate to the vertical. The eye is led upwards to the dome, which is the dominant feature of the whole. Moreover, the arrangement of the rest of the building depends almost entirely on the method adopted to counteract the outward pressure or "thrust" of the dome. Ideally a dome should be supported by equal counter-pressure all round its circumference, as was arranged in the circular domed buildings of the Romans. Properly to support the dome on a square base is a much more difficult task, but one which the Armenians solved in a variety of ways.

Whether the Armenians were really masters of the mechanics of building, as Strzygowski seems to think, must be doubted in view of Baltrušaitis' writings. Undoubtedly their domes were generally very adequately supported, by buttresses of various forms. But they made little effort to economise masonry, and the enormously thick walls of many Armenian churches contain "negative" areas, either hollow or filled with useless masonry, which serve no constructive purpose at all. Armenian plans are often excessively complicated, so as to give the impression of geometrical designs, rather than the foundations of buildings in three dimensions. Moreover, there is commonly a complete lack of correspondence between the plans of the outside and the inside; the one may give no idea whatever of the other. Thus plain rectangular exteriors may mask an interior of extraordinary and apparently unnecessary complexity. Apses may be hidden entirely within the thickness of walls. An outside square may contain an eight-lobed space, a circle a quatrefoil, and so on (p. 83).

This, however, does not mean that the Armenians were ignorant of constructive principles. All the many types of "centralised" church show adequate and logical provision for the support of the dome. They came near to an ideal arrangement in certain churches by providing

eight points of resistance, four points on the axes, and four on the
diagonals (B, p. 83). The resistance was provided by structures called
by Strzygowski "niche-" or "apse-buttresses". They sometimes project
conspicuously outside, which is unusual in any form of Byzantine architecture. Some churches appear to have a projecting apse on all four
sides; these are the axial niche-buttresses [Plate 82]. In others they do
not actually extend beyond the straight lines of the plan, but their
position is marked by two recesses or "splayed niches", one on either
side of the buttresses [Plate 83, 1]. These recesses, as all authorities
admit, are an Armenian invention never applied elsewhere. Apart from
their decorative value, they effect a certain economy in masonry just
where bulk is not required—a process, however, never carried far by
the Armenians. From the apse-buttress, used in Armenia as a purely
constructive expedient, Strzygowski derives the semi-dome of Byzantine
architecture (which still serves the same purpose) and the apse of
Romanesque, in which style the function is no longer primarily
structural.

An astonishing variety of centralised plans occurs in Armenia, where
Strzygowski has made a close study of them. A very early type is the
"apse-buttressed square", which has four principal axial buttresses,
and sometimes four lesser ones in the corners (A, B, p. 83). Of this
type are the Church of St Ripsima at Echmiadzin in Armenia, and the
Djuari church on top of a steep hill opposite Mtskhet in Georgia. They
date from the sixth and seventh centuries [Plates 82; 83, 1].

From the apse-buttressed square was perhaps derived the quatrefoil,
in which the buttresses usurp the whole wall space, and unite at their
edges, so that no flat wall remains. Some small chapels, though round
or square outside, show the quatrefoil internally (D, p. 83). A rarer
plan is the multifoil, in which the dome is supported by either six or
eight small apse-buttresses, the building appearing externally either
round or polygonal. Several survive in the ancient city of Ani.

It was probably the demand for greater space that led to further
modifications of the centralised plan. Churches were enlarged by the

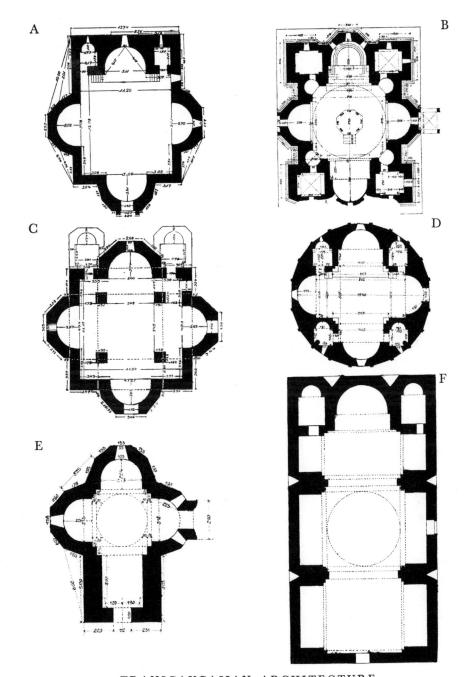

TRANSCAUCASIAN ARCHITECTURE

A. Apse-buttressed square (Mastara). B. Plan of the Djuari Church at Mtskhet, in type similar to A but with additional apse-buttresses in the corners and other complications. C. Apse-buttressed square with free internal pillars (Bagaran). D. Quatrefoil contained in a circle (Khtskonk). E. Trefoil (Alaman). F. Hall church (Shirakavan). This type of plan was used in the churches of Sanaïn and Haghpat.

introduction of barrel vaults[1] to intervene between the base of the dome and the supporting buttresses. The walls were thus made to retreat from the dome, which had to be supported by four pillars standing free in the central space.

When the church remains symmetrical, as at Bagaran (C, p. 83), the result is a square plan with three aisles; otherwise described, a square with "inscribed" Greek cross. It was to this type of plan (omitting the four apse-buttresses, which became unnecessary in the presence of the barrel vaults) that belonged the ninth century "New Church" (Nea) built by Basil I at Constantinople. This church no longer exists. It was sharply distinguished from the other sort of cruciform plan (typified by the lost church of the Apostles at Constantinople and St Mark at Venice) by the position of the domes, which were placed not on the arms of the cross but over the corners; also by the absence of projecting arms. This "Nea" type was widely used in the Balkans, and became the universal form in Russia; its origin in Armenia, according to Strzygowski's suggestion, would therefore be a matter of great interest if established.

The five-aisled church of Mokvi in Abkhazia was mentioned in the account of Kiev (p. 15), but since this type seems most likely to have been introduced directly from Constantinople, and is in no way characteristic of Transcaucasian architecture, more need not be said of it here.

By lengthening the western barrel-vault in a church of the Bagaran type, or by replacing the western buttress of a "niche-buttressed square" by such a vault, a long-naved "trefoil" plan results. In the former case there will be aisles in the nave; in the latter none (E, p. 83). These plans exist in Armenia, and Strzygowski claims for them a great influence in Europe, where they occur in widely separated areas (see p. 100).

By extending both eastern and western ends of the cruciform plan, or, picturing the matter in another way, by combining the square-

---

[1] Vaults of semi-cylindrical form, as distinct from the cross or groined vaults which are used universally in the later mediaeval styles of the West.

domed church with the basilica, that form of church was produced which in the tenth and eleventh centuries became the most popular and widespread in both Armenia and Georgia (F, p. 83).

3. ARMENIA, TENTH AND ELEVENTH CENTURIES

The latter type of church above described as most characteristic of both Caucasian countries made its first appearance in the eighth century, but was not widely used until the tenth. Its form is certainly well described as that of a basilica on which is imposed a transept and cupola —whether or not the builders really intended to combine the "centralised" and basilican plans. Such churches have undergone an increase in length, and a reduction in the relative importance of the dome, which takes them definitely out of the category of "centralised" buildings. Sometimes they have two pairs of free-standing pillars as at Bagaran, or more, giving a nave with aisles. But in the plan most freely used by the Armenians in their later period of building this arrangement was superseded. The four principal supports, instead of standing free in the middle of the church, were applied to the walls, so that the aisles disappeared as such, remaining only in the form of recesses. The result is what Strzygowski calls the "hall-church" (F, p. 83). It is distinguished by the "spacial unity" of the interior, a character always sought after by the Armenians, with whom interiors encumbered by pillars were never appreciated. It is this plan that was used in the principal churches of the monasteries at Sanaïn and Haghpat.

In the early period of their building activity, already described, the Armenians concentrated their efforts on structure alone; as has been seen, they elaborated a quite remarkable variety in the plans of their churches. But little effort was made to decorate them; the great problem of how best to enclose a space was enough to engross the entire attention of the architects. Ornamental detail was not, indeed, entirely absent, but it assumed nothing like its great prominence in later times.

A window of the seventh-century church at Pthni has lively figures of Persian origin, and medallions with heads of saints [Plates 89, 90].

It was during the later period now in question—the tenth and eleventh centuries—that the Armenians began to pay serious attention to the embellishment of their churches. They had by this time settled down to a satisfactory plan, that of the "hall-church", and further development was in the direction of increasing elaboration of the surface, whether inside or out. It was now that the geometrical designs so characteristic of Armenia began to assume a foremost place in architectural decoration, and this is attributable, in part at least, to contact with the Arabs, who now had control of a great part of the country.

Most of the abundant remains of Armenian architecture are to be found among the many ancient monasteries which are scattered widely over the hills and valleys of this mountainous country. Mostly long since deserted, they are a sad relic of the once flourishing life and culture of the most unfortunate of peoples. Sometimes these monasteries lie high in the mountains, approachable only by rocky paths and inaccessible to traffic on wheels. Often the groups of monastic buildings, including several cone-roofed churches and chapels with their entrance halls and bell tower, all against a background of mighty hills, offer to the traveller a composition both striking and picturesque, and one highly characteristic of this interesting region [Plate 84].

The most pleasing of lesser architectural features in the Armenian style is the blind arcade, which appears here at an extremely early date. It is freely used as a wall decoration, and also on the drum which supports the dome. Strzygowski finds the home of this arcade in northern Iran, and supposes that it came thence with the domed square which is the fundamental unit in Armenian architecture. An early example is provided by the larger church at Sanaïn, built in 961. Here the semi-columns are double (at the corners multiple), and are surmounted by capitals correspondingly divided, and in very great variety [Plates 85-7].

Armenian doorways and other arches are a most interesting subject of study. Primitively they were simple and round, but other forms were evolved showing a striking parallel with, and in some cases forestalling, Romanesque and Gothic developments in the West [Plate 89, 4]. Doorways are sometimes recessed in two or three orders, as in the Romanesque style, or are encased in several concentric bands of ornament, not necessarily divided into columns and arch. Very commonly, in doors as in windows, the logical function of the semi-column is abandoned; it may be turned through a right angle at the bottom, where one expects a base, or even carried across horizontally to meet its fellow on the other side. The pointed arch, either simple or tapering in the form of an ogee, appears as early as the eleventh century, before its use in western Europe [Plate 88, 3, 4]. Other forms of arch in Armenia were evidently adopted from the Mahommedans; such are the horseshoe, and the trefoil, which appears on the drum of a little chapel at Haghpat [Plate 87, 1].

Windows, like doorways, affect a great variety of forms. They are often encased in single or paired semi-columns, and may be divided into lights. In a very common form the archivolt does not rest directly on the impost,[1] but is turned outwards at the springing to right and left [Plate 85, 1]. The same form may be retained, even though there be no impost at all.

An essential character of Armenian decoration is the use of purely geometrical patterns, which reach a very high pitch of complexity, excelled only by those elaborated by the Mahommedans in the later Middle Ages. Such ornament is freely applied to the frames of doors and windows, to arcades, and the bases and capitals of pillars. But it reaches its fullest development on the Armenian memorial stone or *hachkar* [Plates 90, 1; 91]. These stones are strewn on Armenian soil in tremendous numbers, but are quite absent from Georgia. Their central feature is usually a cross of remarkable form, the ends of its four arms

---

[1] The upper member of a capital or series of capitals or any corresponding structure on which the arch of an opening rests.

being bifid, somewhat as in a Maltese cross. Around it are disposed a series of panels filled with interlaced designs, of which no two in a single stone, or even in several together, are alike. Their variety is infinite, and their richness altogether bewildering. Arising from the extremity of the long lower limb of the cross are commonly two curious extensions with spiral tips. They take the place of what appears in many Byzantine and Italian crosses as a definitely vegetable subject, perhaps with some symbolic meaning.

The Armenian sculptor-geometricians seem to have lavished their greatest efforts on these extraordinary stones. Wealthy persons often had them made as future memorials to themselves, and in the hope that by so doing they would find greater favour with the Creator in the life to come.

Baltrušaitis has made a minute study of Transcaucasian interlacements, and he finds certain prevailing differences between those of Armenia and Georgia. The former tend to be more diffuse; the latter more concentrated. In Georgia certain recognisable geometrical forms emerge from the meshwork, whereas in Armenia all individual form is lost in a maze of strands which can be looked at only as a whole. But to understand the matter rightly reference must be made to Baltrušaitis' magnificent book.

There appears at first sight a surprising correspondence between the interlacing patterns on Armenian stones, and those of European countries—those, most notably, of the Scottish cross-slabs, and the high crosses of Ireland. Yet, in spite of occasional identity in the designs, a detailed study reveals important differences. In Celtic interlaced work the basis of the pattern generally shows through quite plainly as a simple plait, the lines showing a tendency to run diagonally over the space covered. In Armenian designs, on the other hand, the basic plait is seldom visible, though Baltrušaitis claims that even the most complex among them are developed from it, fundamentally. In Armenia the plait was treated somewhat otherwise than in the Celtic countries, and the process of elaboration was carried further. By breaking and reconnecting the strands in various ways the plait was made to yield systems of interlocking circles and polygons; these were then used as the scaffolding on which to build up intertwined patterns more complex still [Plate 91].

It is a question to what extent Armenian and Celtic ornament are independent in their derivation, whether they have drawn from some common source, or have had some mutual influence. More will be said about this when describing the supposed influence of Armenia in the Western countries (p. 101).

The sculpture of human and animal subjects occurs in Armenia, though to what extent it was intended as decoration is not always clear; its intention was sometimes symbolic or commemorative. The style of this sculpture, which is essentially naturalistic rather than formal, shows its origin to have been quite different from that of the geometrical ornament just described. It seems to have come, in fact, from that union of Hellenistic and ancient Asiatic art which was mentioned on a previous page.

Many of the subjects found in Armenia are common to the arts of most of the peoples of western Asia, and some have their origin in the ancient civilisations of Mesopotamia. Among these widespread subjects are the lion "passant" with head turned so as to appear full-face; lions in pairs, affronted or back to back; pursuits of one creature by another, and combats; horsemen and other figures, often in symmetrical pairs on either side of a tree; fantastic winged quadrupeds and birds. In Armenia liberties were often taken with the standard subjects; lions might be replaced by bears, goats, and other local animals, or by entirely imaginary creatures.

On the whole, sculpture of this kind is not abundant either in Armenia or Georgia. Where it occurs, the subjects are often scattered singly and somewhat at random [Plates 86, 1; 102, 2]. One altogether exceptional building must, however, be mentioned—the church of Akhtamar on an island in Lake Van. In this area, somewhat far removed from the main centre of Armenian building, the architects must have felt very strongly the influence of the arts of Mesopotamia and Sassanian Persia. The walls are covered with beasts and birds in great variety, some true to life, others fantastic; there are also saints and scriptural subjects, and many of the carvings are enclosed in medallions.[1] Pthni, near Erivan, shows a certain number of comparable carvings [Plates 89, 90]. These buildings were mentioned before in connection with the Russian churches of Vladimir, and especially the cathedral of Yuriev Polski, which have many similar subjects and were possibly built under Armenian influence.

The Armenian and Georgian styles, like the Russian, are distinguished from the generality of Byzantine architecture in their possession of separate bell towers. These are not constant in form, but they generally terminate above in an open spirelet, consisting of a ring of columns supporting a conical roof. This was apparently an Armenian invention, though Rivoira thinks it may have been suggested by a form of minaret. A very striking tower distinctively Armenian in type stands at Haghpat. Here the corners of the tower are recessed below, and the transition to the square above is made by external squinches bridging each recess [Plate 104].

One of the many misfortunes brought upon architecture in the train of political strife is the present Russo-Turkish frontier, which cuts through the very centre of Armenia, just where the remains of its ancient architecture lie thickest on the ground. The walls of Ani, once a great city and capital of Armenia, lie a few hundred yards from the frontier in the territory of the less hospitable Government, and this veritable museum of Armenian architecture, with much of the best work it has produced, is unapproachable.

The cathedral of Ani is worthy (if, indeed, it still exists) of far greater renown than actually surrounds it. Outside, it is a fine specimen of building in the typical Armenian manner, with blind arcades of great beauty. But inside it bears the semblance of a Gothic cathedral such as

[1] Illustrations of this church can be found in Strzygowski's *Origin of Christian Church Art* and in Rivoira's *Moslem Architecture*.

western Europe might have seen two centuries later. Pairs of clustered columns support a high pointed vault, and on either side is an aisle with narrow pointed arches like those of the "Early English" style. It is assuredly a striking example of parallel evolution, even if all idea of a connection with the Gothic must be dismissed.[1]

The Armenian kingdom had attained to great power and prosperity, and to a distinguished place in the artistic world, under the Bagratid dynasty in the tenth and eleventh centuries. But in the middle of the eleventh century the country was overrun by the Byzantines; not long after again by the Seljuk Turks. Thus a powerful and independent Armenia ceased to be, but building continued in a small way until the first Mongol invasion early in the thirteenth century. In the twelfth century Armenia fell under the rule of the Georgian Bagratids—an offshoot of the Armenian house—and from that time the Georgians played the leading part in Transcaucasia. In their hands architecture took a somewhat new form, better described as Georgian than as Armenian.

4. GEORGIA

The architectures of Georgia and Armenia are not sharply distinguished. Chubinashvili, who emphasises their independence, says that the differences between these two styles are of the same order as those which separate (for instance) the Romanesque of France and Germany. Most people would perhaps hardly see so great a difference. The general aspect of Georgian buildings is nevertheless distinctive, and this is due mainly to peculiarities in the carved ornament, and its distribution over the building, as will be presently explained.

The oldest churches built on Georgian soil—those of Chubinashvili's "Early Christian" period—have been mentioned under the heading of Armenia, and may have been the work of Armenians. Here I shall

[1] Illustrations in Lynch's *Armenia*.

mention mainly those buildings erected presumably by Georgian architects in the brightest period of Georgian civilisation from the tenth to the thirteenth centuries (the middle of Chubinashvili's "mediaeval" period, which lasts from the ninth to the fifteenth). In the latter part of this time Armenia became part of the Georgian kingdom and the architecture of the Georgians, directly based on the Armenian style, spread again over parts of Armenia in a different form. Georgia is to be regarded, however, as the first architectural province of Armenia; moreover, it was more especially through Georgia that the influence of Armenian architecture became felt in western Europe.

All the principal buildings of the Georgian kingdom from about the tenth century onwards were of the type combining basilica and centralised church, having what may be described as a nave and choir, transepts, and a cupola over the crossing. Often, especially in the larger churches, there were several pairs of free-standing pillars in the nave, giving an aisle on either side.

As in Armenia, geometrical ornament—largely interlaced work—here plays an important part in church decoration. But it has a different character from that of Armenia. Henri Focillon, in his preface to Baltrušaitis' book, summarises the matter in these words:

L'entrelacs géorgien donne un décor homogène. Les éléments bien serrés respectent l'unité des formes. . . . Les décorateurs arméniens procèdent, au contraire, par entre-croisement;[1] la puissance de la spéculation analytique les amène à décomposer les thèmes avec une inflexible sécheresse, et l'unité des formes se trouve rigoureusement détruite au profit de la lisibilité des éléments. Ces différences sont également sensibles dans le relief: tandis qu'en Arménie, il se trouve réduit à un pur graphisme, accentué par de minces canaux d'ombre, la facture géorgienne est plus simple, moins linéaire et plus colorée.

In other words, the Armenians showed a near approach to the methods of the Mahommedans in spreading and decomposing the elements of their ornament; the Georgians approached the methods of

[1] A process which reduces designs to a diffuse network of rectilinear strands crossing at a constant angle.

Romanesque architects in concentrating them. Georgian architecture provides, in fact, a link between the very dissimilar architectures of the Christian West, and of Islam.

A more striking character of Georgian decoration is found, however, in the widespread use of a leaf-like or "palmette" ornament in association with interlaced designs. Its origin and use were originally quite distinct from those of the interlacement; it is the contribution, according to Strzygowski, of the central Asiatic Mongols to the world repertory of art forms (see p. 78). The delightful story of the evolution of this palmette in Georgian architecture is told in Baltrušaitis' book, but is too complex to be followed here. It lost, eventually, its own individuality, being merged in and subordinated to the interlacement, which is always the dominant motive in Transcaucasian decoration. Here an interesting comparison may be made with Romanesque detail. This often uses the same elements exactly—an interlacement, and a palmette; but it associates them in a different way. In the Romanesque style it is the palmette that controls the interlacement, which is a subordinate feature without rights of its own.

Figure sculpture, too, finds its place in the scheme of Georgian decoration; there are human and animal subjects in constant use similar to those of Armenia. Baltrušaitis finds that even this form of decoration is subject to geometrical laws. The forms given to men and creatures depend not so much on their actual shape as on the space they have to occupy. A close approach in style is here discernible to the work of Romanesque sculptors in the West, where also many of the same subjects were in regular use.

Georgian architecture, even more pronouncedly than that of Armenia, shows various "atectonic" features which Baltrušaitis brings forward in making comparisons, unfavourable to Georgia, with Romanesque architecture in the West. These characters, he considers, betray a want of true architectural sense on the part of the architects; a failure to picture their buildings as an organic whole; a lack of understanding of the proper relation of form to function. The builders were geometricians, masons, decorators—their point of view was that of the jeweller, not of the architect.

I have mentioned earlier the peculiar character of many Armenian and Georgian plans, in which the outside form hides rather than reproduces the complex arrangements of the interior. In the actual structure of the walls and vaults lies a similar deception. The core of the walls is a mass of rubble imbedded in concrete, and this is covered over and completely hidden by a facing of stones accurately fitted together without mortar. These stones, however, do not take the form of regular blocks, as they would have to do if intrinsic parts of the structure. They are of all sizes, and often most irregular in shape. Windows and small doorways, far from being built up of independent pieces, are often cut out of a few large blocks of stone. Arches and pillars are similarly moulded in the general surface of the facing. Decorative schemes pay no heed to the position of individual stones, but spread widely over the surface as on a wall of plaster or stucco.

In architectural details the primitive structural value of many forms is lost. The cushion capital degenerates into a sphere. Semi-columns, whose ends are indistinguishable, may lie horizontally under the windows. At Gelati are several examples of such "atectonic" forms. The north portal of the principal church [Plate 103] has on either side a curious column whose upper and lower extremities are of the same design, the one resting on a square base, the other supporting a square capital. These columns serve no useful purpose. On the south side of the same church is a decorative arcade further illustrating this theme [Plate 99]. Here again capitals and bases are reduced to the same form, one in any case inappropriate for supporting a superincumbent weight. Ornamental sculpture, instead of being applied to the capitals, has deserted these in favour of the ends of the column, which in the Romanesque style are generally left to fulfil their function unadorned.

Georgian detail is spread like a garment over the blank surface of walls, quite without relation to the "tectonics" of the building. The nucleus of a decorative scheme is most often a window, whose opening is reduced to a mere slit through the extension and elaboration of the frame. This is commonly prolonged upwards and expanded above as a huge cross; or it may connect with decorative areas of other shapes, below or to the sides. Associated with the principal pattern are generally plaques and bosses of various forms, and sculptured beasts and human figures may be worked into the scheme [Plates 93, 1; 100, 2].

In defence of a style which, in spite of the defects enumerated, does produce an extremely satisfactory effect, one may well ask whether any unique merit attaches to the methods followed by the Romanesque builders. Is there any abstract reason for subordinating ornament to structural mechanics, for making of decoration something integral, expressive of structure, rather than something extraneous, which ignores it? Whatever the answer to this question, the sure fact remains that these ancient churches of Armenia and Georgia give an impression of monumentality, combined with grace, which is seldom surpassed.

The earliest churches of the "mediaeval" stage in Georgian architecture—those dating from the end of the eighth or the ninth century—are comparatively simple and plain. Their plans are rectangular and show no sign externally of the apses, even in the form of niches at the eastern end. Some of them nevertheless have a special charm owing to their extraordinary position. Such is the church of the Safar Monastery, perched on a precipitous hillside.[1]

A similar church, of later date, is that of Tsminda Sameba, on the very top of a high hill under the great peak of Mount Kazbek, overlooking Kazbek village [Plates 92, 93]. Here, however, the doorways and the walls above them are ornamented with geometrical designs. Adjoining the church is a bell tower of typical Georgian form [Plate 105, 1]. One of its windows has two carved beasts, of quite anomalous shape and unsymmetrical in position, climbing on the rim of the archivolt [Plate 102, 2]. This church is surrounded by the remains of fortifications, and appears to have been a place of refuge, used also for the

[1] Illustrations of this and other Georgian churches are reproduced in a paper by Mr W. E. D. Allen in the *Geographical Journal* for August, 1929.

safe keeping of church valuables in times of danger. This is one of the most northerly churches in the Georgian style, for it lies some miles north of the main Caucasian watershed near the military road between Tiflis and Vladikavkaz.

At Mtskhet, the ancient capital of Georgia, lying on the Aragva about twenty miles north of Tiflis [Plate 101, 2], are two splendid examples of the later Georgian style, as well as the seventh-century Djuari church which crowns the top of a hill on the opposite side of the river (p. 82). The earlier of the two churches in the village is the cathedral, an imposing building of the eleventh century. This is the largest structure in all Georgia, and is unique in that not only the nave, but also the transepts, have a roof of which the slope is interrupted, as in the vaulted basilica. The walls of the cathedral are arcaded, and at the east end two side arches enclose the recesses which mark the position of the apses. At the west end of the church is an extension with somewhat lower roof than the nave, and this in its turn has a massive porch. Some of the windows are surrounded with elaborate sculpturing, and a number of grotesque beasts are scattered about the walls [Plates 94, 95].

Almost contemporary with Mtskhet cathedral is the monastery of Gelati near Kutaïs in western Georgia. It is beautifully placed high on a hill-side among the foothills of the Caucasus, in view of the snowy peaks of the central range [Plate 101, 1]. Enclosed within a high wall are the monastic buildings, including two churches, a bell tower [Plate 105, 2], and a little chapel built over an open vault which covers a well-head [Plate 102, 1]. The older and larger of the two churches, dating from the later eleventh and early twelfth centuries, is one of the most dignified buildings in Georgia. Its proportions are very perfect, and much of the ornamentation exceptionally pleasing. Adding considerably to its beauty are the three eastern apses, which here project freely, an unusual arrangement in the Caucasus. They are decorated with a slender arcade of great perfection; other arcades are found on the walls, and on the drum supporting the cone-shaped dome [Plates 95, 96, 98, 99].

The second church at Mtskhet, in the convent of Samtavro, at once betrays its later date (twelfth century) by the greater richness of its carved ornament, especially around the windows of the drum, and on the ends of the transepts. This church is considerably smaller than the cathedral, which it resembles, however, in the arcading of the walls, and in the recesses at the east end [Plate 97]. A fine belfry dating from the fifteenth or sixteenth century rises from a corner of the convent wall [Plate 105, 3].

During the thirteenth century the tendency in Georgia was to increasing elaboration of detail, until "tout l'édifice disparaît derrière la broderie ornementale". But in the later centuries of Georgian history the resources of the country did not admit of such elaboration, and a reversion to simpler types is seen in the few churches built.

Invasions and plunderings were the lot of Georgia no less than of Armenia through a great part of her history. Persians of various dynasties, Arabs, Turks and Mongols all penetrated repeatedly from the Asiatic side, to say nothing of invasions from the West. Not all these events proved inimical in the long run to artistic progress, indeed some were most fortunate from this very point of view. But the first Mongol incursion in 1235, bringing to a close a period of tranquillity and great artistic achievement, was indeed the beginning of the end. After this date there was little architectural activity in Georgia; less still after the second invasion in the following century, under Timur (Tamerlane) with his almost unparalleled frenzy for destruction.

An example of later Georgian architecture is the church in the fortress of Ananur on the Georgian military road, built about the sixteenth century [Plate 100, 1, 2]. Churches of a still more recent period show little of interest. They are built of brick, a material almost unknown in mediaeval Caucasian architecture, and they show a tendency to heightening of the proportions shared by the Russians in the later stages of their architectural history [Plate 100, 3].

Thus Georgia, artistically speaking, almost ceased to be after the thirteenth century, the very period when architecture in the West was

experiencing a most fruitful expansion and that of Russia, eclipsed for
the moment, was preparing a great Renaissance. But Georgia, unlike
Armenia, retained her political entity right on through the centuries,
until, in 1803, the sovereignty of this ancient kingdom passed at last
from the long-lived House of the Bagratids to the Romanovs of Russia.

5. SPREAD OF CAUCASIAN INFLUENCE WESTWARDS

It was noted above that the question of Armenian and Georgian influence in the West is extremely controversial. Even the most conservative students of the subject do, however, admit some such influence.
Rivoira writes: "It was in Armenia that domes with high drums were
first used in churches, and decorated with blank arcades in which the
arches spring from slender shafts"; thus implying the possibility of the
high drum having spread westwards from Armenia. And further:
"The Armenian use of continuous blank arcading of elegant form had
an influence not only in the East, but also in the West, and in Italy itself,
which had given birth to this form of decoration".

To Strzygowski, however, Rivoira's chief opponent on the architectural battlefield, is due the theory which gives Armenia a central
place in the history of European architecture, and almost the whole
share in transplanting the dome over a square bay from its home in
northern Iran into Europe. He finds the various Armenian plans
spreading to every country in southern and western Europe. Students
with a more balanced point of view allow more—as Strzygowski himself
once did—to the fertile architectural schools of Asia Minor.

The means of dispersal of influences from western Asia and the east
Mediterranean were various. Communications by water played an
important part, for trade with the west of Europe was active, and commercial colonies of eastern people were established in every port and
many inland cities throughout the Middle Ages. It is, however, more

easy to understand the spread of decorative and iconographic subjects than of architecture itself. The former could be carried far and wide in the form of textiles, manuscripts, ivories, enamel and metal-work—all objects easily portable, and which were in fact dispersed in vast quantity all over the western countries.

For the spread of architectural forms and methods the presence of persons acquainted with the country of origin and themselves with an understanding of architecture is required—conditions not so easily fulfilled. But there seems to have been provision enough for the active operation of Armenian influence in the West. At such cities as Constantinople, Jerusalem and Ravenna, and in the Balkan countries, there were Armenian colonies from very early times. The Byzantine emperor Basil I (ninth century) was himself an Armenian.

Strzygowski's theory in its extreme form would make Italy and the whole Byzantine Empire, even as early as the fifth century, practically an architectural colony of Armenia. All buildings showing the dome over a square must be included, not excepting the fifth-century mausoleum of Galla Placidia at Ravenna, and other early Christian buildings of north Italy.

Strzygowski's view of the origin of St Sophia at Constantinople is thus expressed in his *Origin of Christian Church Art*:

In conception the church is purely Armenian; a central dome over a square plan is supported by semi-domes abutting on the sides of the square. It is true that the Armenian niche-buttresses are replaced on the North and South by vaults between massive piers which allowed the introduction of galleries; but the architects of the Ottoman conquerors were quick to recognise the original design, and, in the huge mosques built in imitation of the church, to restore the Armenian four-lobed plan.

This view is stoutly disputed by those who maintain that no Armenian influence could have been felt in the West until after the iconoclastic period (eighth and ninth centuries).

The plan of St Sophia is generally looked upon (that is, if attributed to eastern influences at all) as derived from a "domed basilica" of

Anatolian origin. The type, whether originating in Asia Minor or in Armenia, has other representatives in the West. Such are St Irene at Constantinople, and later churches in Greece (Philippi) and Bulgaria (a ruinous one at Pirdop, and St Sophia at Sofia, which still stands).

The Greek cross plan typified by Basil I's "Nea" is usually regarded as the logical outcome of the principles embodied in the "domed basilica", though Strzygowski, as was mentioned before (p. 84) finds its origin in Armenia, and Basil's Armenian nationality lends colour to this view. This type is widely represented in the Balkans and in Russia; it became, in fact, the standard plan in the Greek Orthodox Church.

The Armenian quatrefoil is found in Italy, as in the baptisteries of Biella and Galliano; among the most ancient churches of the Czechs; at Cracow in the south of Poland; in the "Red Ruin" near Plovdiv (Philippopolis) in Bulgaria. The quatrefoil reappears in France at Mont-majour (Provence), while at Germigny-des-Prés (on the Loire, near Orleans) is an exact reproduction of the Armenian apse-buttressed square with free central pillars, dating from the ninth century. The latter type occurs also at Milan (San Satiro). In both cases the plan closely resembles that of Bagaran in Armenia (C, p. 83).

Both quatrefoil and trefoil are used in Greece at Athos and elsewhere, and the latter, at a much later time, became frequent in the Balkans. In the eleventh century the trefoil had reached Germany—it is a characteristic plan in the Romanesque style of that country.

It is an interesting fact that several of these plans, including, most conspicuously, the apse-buttressed square, appear unmistakably in some of Leonardo da Vinci's architectural drawings. It seems to show that this master of all arts did not ignore the suggestions that Armenia had to offer in the field of architectural design.

Various churches in western Europe are commonly described as copies of early Christian and Byzantine originals in Italy. Thus St Front at Périgueux—one specimen of a whole class of domed churches in France—would be a reproduction of St Mark at Venice; the cathedral of Aix-la-Chapelle a copy of the octagonal San Vitale at Ravenna.

Strzygowski sees in these the influence of eastern models in the development of which Armenia had taken her part. St Mark and San Vitale were not prototypes, but marked simply stages in the passage westwards of Asiatic ideas, just as did many of the monuments of Constantinople.

Of first importance, according to Strzygowski, in the westward extension of Armenian ideas in building, were the migrations of the Goths. In the course of their wanderings they travelled from the south of Russia westwards through the Balkans to Bohemia, Germany, and France, even as far as Spain. These Goths had made contact with the peoples of western Asia by their raids into Transcaucasia and Asia Minor, and they are supposed to have carried Persian and Armenian architects in their train on their migrations to western Europe. It was they who brought these eastern plans across Europe, who introduced the dome, and had much to do with the establishment of the vault. To them was largely due the initiation of the "Romanesque" style which had so splendid a success in western Europe. Such are the theories with which Strzygowski confronts Rivoira, who would derive all mediaeval styles from the Lombardic basilica.

Strzygowski sees no difficulty in carrying the influence of the Goths as far west as Britain, and in thus explaining the appearance of analogies to Syrian and to Transcaucasian art in the early stonework of these islands. But he emphasises also the feasibility of other routes in the transmission of artistic ideas from western Asia: the sea way via the Mediterranean (which was undoubtedly in use as early as the seventh and eighth centuries) and the way over land via Russia and Scandinavia. A Scandinavian connection is in any case manifest in the early art of Britain, more especially in the so-called zoomorphic designs which abound both in manuscripts and stone carving.

So far, the influences mentioned would be denied by a majority of architectural historians. But there is stronger evidence for the adoption of Armenian characters, especially in the Balkan countries, at a later period. The connection was first emphasised by Choisy in his descriptions of Serbian and Rumanian churches of the fourteenth to sixteenth centuries.

In Serbia there exists a remarkable series of churches belonging to the end of the fourteenth and beginning of the fifteenth centuries, which, in the arcading of their outside walls, and in details of the carving round their windows, show an almost undoubted influence from the Caucasus. The plan is generally a trefoil, which came no doubt from Athos, whether or not its original home was in Armenia. There are specimens of this style at Krushevats, Lyubostinya, Rudenitsa, Kalenich, Ravanitsa and Lazaritsa, all in the Morava district.[1]

One must turn, however, to Rumania for the most striking example in the Balkans of a church built under Armenian influence; the honour falls, without a doubt, to the cathedral of Curtea de Argeş, among the foothills of the Transylvanian Alps [Plates 106–8]. This singular building stands almost by itself in the world of Byzantine architecture. It has sometimes been associated, entirely without reason, with the Russian style. In reality it shows the influence of the neo-Byzantine tradition as expressed in the aforementioned Serbian churches of a somewhat earlier period. In Rumania itself it has but a single forerunner: the Deal Monastery in the mountains to the north-east of Argeş; and a great many inferior descendants, mostly dating from between the middle of the seventeenth and the beginning of the nineteenth century.

Deal dates from 1500, Argeş from 1517. Both have the trefoil plan —a very prevalent one in Rumania—brought presumably from Athos by way of Serbia. The Wallachian churches, like the Serbian, show a tendency to great external display, at the expense of the interior. In many respects, in fact, the two styles approach each other; but their concurrence is limited by a difference in material, for while the Serbian churches are mainly of brick, the Rumanian material is stone. Nevertheless in general character Argeş comes very near to Krushevats in the Morava valley.

---

[1] Illustrations in Millet, *L'École Grecque dans l'Architecture Byzantine*; Diehl, *Manuel d'Art Byzantin*; Pupin, *South Slav Monuments*.

The church of Argeş has four cupolas. The principal one rises from the trefoil at the eastern end, and another, as broad but lower, stands over the nave. Both are given extra height by the interposition of a square base below the drum. Flanking the second cupola and crowning the western façade are two smaller domes with twisted drums—a feature which might with advantage have been foregone. The exact arrangement of these four cupolas must have cost the architect much thought, and his reward was in unusual success. Indeed one can find no point of view from which they do not appear elegantly grouped, giving an impression entirely pleasing and satisfying. There are few buildings of which this can be said.

Among various features of the Rumanian churches testifying to a Transcaucasian connection, the most conspicuous is the blind arcading of the outside walls. Most Armenian and Georgian churches, and those of the Morava group, have but a single arcade, but in Rumania there are two ranges—one above the other. At Deal both are true arcades with round-headed arches, but at Argeş only the upper tier remains in this form; the lower is transformed into a series of panels. Both the double ranging of the arcades, and the square panelling which may take its place, are characters foreshadowed in Armenia. So, too, is the great twisted cable which at Argeş divides the two tiers. Armenia can provide prototypes of such twisted courses running below arcades—it is true, on a much smaller and simpler scale. One character of the Rumanian arcading separates it absolutely from that of the Romanesque style, or of the Byzantine proper, but connects it closely with Transcaucasia, and especially with Georgia. This is its "atectonic" or non-structural nature. It is not built up of separate stones, but is simply cut in the general surface of the wall. Moreover it pays no heed to the angles of the building, but freely turns corners [Plate 107, 2; and compare Gelati in Georgia, Plate 95, 2]. Yet another common Georgian feature, most unusual in the west: the columns of the arcade have lost their capitals —column and arch form one continuous moulding.

In its details we find that Argeş shows many analogies to Transcaucasian, and many, too, to Mahommedan art. The lavish ornament of the drums recalls Georgia; the elaborate rectangular window frames are an Armenian character; the ornamental plaques and discs are common to both those countries. The discs are covered with interlacing or arabesque designs; certain of these show a relationship to Transcaucasian work, while others resemble, even to the point of identity, designs on some of the mosques in Cairo.

The western door with its square frame and cusped or denticulated arch may be related either to Armenian or to Moslem prototypes [Plate 107, 1]. The rectangular enclosure at the west end, with its canopied fountain matching the door, at once recalls a Mahommedan rather than a Christian place of worship [Plate 108, 2]. Undoubtedly the architect of Argeş, whatever his nationality, must have known much both of Transcaucasus and of the Mahommedan countries.

Altogether, this is one of the most remarkable of churches, and one showing the possibilities of an eclectic or composite style, drawing its characters from various sources but uniting them in a novel and homogeneous whole.

Taking leave of these diverse styles of the nearer East, one may make some final generalizations in the light of which they show, especially in their later stages, a certain kinship. Thus one observes in decoration an ever increasing attention to superficial and extraneous detail; this suggests a comparison with the baroque phase into which passed the architecture of the Renaissance, or that last, and to some minds degenerate, stage of Moorish architecture typified by the Alhambra of Granada. It seems true to say that this insistence on detail involved a certain sacrifice of the monumental quality. Moreover undue heightening and exclusive attention to the exterior deprived most later buildings of that completeness and balance which distinguishes the mediaeval architecture of western Europe. Yet the eastern churches gained thereby a picturesqueness and charm by no means to be despised as architectural qualities, and they abundantly repay that interest and study which is due to all monuments of human history.

PLATES

Plate 1. KIEV AND NOVGOROD, Eleventh century

1. *Kiev. Apses of the Cathedral of St Sophia.* 1036

No other part of the exterior retains any approach to its original form. These five eastern apses correspond to the five aisles into which the church is divided. They are ornamented with rows of arches, mostly blind; and the central apse has long shafts. The two buttresses are subsequent (see also Pl. 57, 3).

Here there are only three apses, and the shafts decorating the central apse have lost their capitals.

2. *Novgorod. East end of St Sophia.* 1045–52

Plate 2. NOVGOROD, Eleventh century

Cathedral of St Sophia. 1045–52. South side

The earliest and largest of the Novgorod churches. Broad buttress-like projections on the walls mark the position of the principal lines of vaulting in the building. There are six domes: the group of five over the eastern part of the church is arranged in the way universal in Russia; the large sixth dome covers an extra bay at the western end.

Plate 3. NOVGOROD, Twelfth century

1. *St Nicholas the Wonder-Worker.* 1113

In these twelfth-century Novgorod churches three apses are retained, but the number of domes tends to be reduced. Here the extra cupola surmounting the large central dome is a later addition.

2. *Church of the Nativity of the Virgin.* 1116

Remarkable for the round tower at north-west corner, carrying one of the two extra western domes.

3. *Sobor in the Monastery of St George.* 1119–30

…as an asymmetrical plan similar to that of the last; …e north-west dome is carried by a rectangular …mpartment not repeated on the south.

4. *Church of the Saviour.* 1198

In this later church the side apses are seen much reduced; in the thirteenth century they disappeared altogether. The interior has thirteenth-century frescoes admirably preserved.

Plate 4. NOVGOROD, Fourteenth and Fifteenth centuries

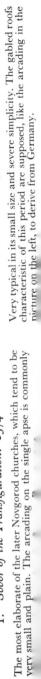

2. *Church of St Simon.* 1468

Very typical in its small size and severe simplicity. The gabled roofs characteristic of this period are supposed, like the arcading in the picture on the left, to derive from Germany.

1. *Sobor of the Transfiguration.* 1374

The most elaborate of the later Novgorod churches, which tend to be very small and plain. The arcading on the single apse is commonly

Plate 5. NOVGOROD, Sixteenth century

1. *Church of Procopius the Martyr.* 1529

Flat pilasters and ogee arches characterise the sixteenth century at Novgorod. It was a period of rapid decline, and few churches were built.

2. *Church of SS. Boris and Gleb.* 1536

An unusual building, gaining picturesqueness from the elaborate gabling of the roofs. A reversion to the five-domed plan is seen.

Plate 6. PSKOV, Twelfth and Fifteenth centuries

1. *Sobor of the Transfiguration.* 1156

This church has two much reduced side apses, but they are hidden in the photograph. The north and south walls each have two blind arches; one tall, the other low.

2. *Bell Tower of the same. Later*

This shows part of the same north wall as appears in the adjoining picture. The attached bell-arcade or bell-cot is almost the most primitive conceivable. It is much later than the church.

3. *Church of the Epiphany.* 1444

Shows the usual tripartite division of the walls, and ornamental arcading on the apse.

4. *Church of St Parmenius*(?). 1444

Here a gallery surrounds the church—a feature at the time peculiar to Pskov. A typical entrance-way with stumpy pillars gives access to the gallery.

Plate 7. BELL-COTS OF THE PSKOV TYPE

1. *Pskov. Bell-cot of St Parmenius.* **1444**
simple specimen with five open arches of varying
idth. The ropes, by which the clappers are worked,
'e seen hanging from the bells.

2. *Novgorod. Bell-cot attached to the
Cathedral of St Sophia.* **1439**
An earlier, but more finished and elaborate speci-
men, with well-developed cupola.

. *Pskov. Bell-cot of the Epiphany
Church.* **1495**
'ther simple example with four arches,
somewhat more prominent cross.

4. *Rostov Veliki. A later type derived from the
Bell-cots of Pskov.* **1690**
Bells were often housed in structures of this kind, derived from
Pskov, up to the seventeenth century. This one stands adjacent to
the cathedral in the Kremlin of Rostov (see Pl. 21, 1).

Plate 8. VLADIMIR, Twelfth century

1. *Church of the Intercession on the River Nerl.* 1166

One of the most attractive churches ever built in Russia (see frontispiece). The material, as in all Vladimir churches, is

2. *The same. North side*

Especially characteristic of the Vladimir churches are the arcades on all four sides. On the north, south and west a space is left above the windows, and this tends to be filled with sculpture (see Pls. 10–13).

Plate 9.   VLADIMIR, Twelfth century

Cathedral of the Assumption.   1189

The largest building in this style, and long considered the crowning achievement of Russian architecture. Served in the fifteenth century as a model for the Cathedral of the Assumption in the Kremlin at Moscow.

Plate 10. VLADIMIR, Twelfth century

Church of St Dmitri. 1194–7. *West front*

This church is an enlarged and elaborated edition of the Intercession on the Nerl. Its dome happens to retain the 'helmet' form, which marks a stage in the development of the Russian dome intermediate between the hemisphere and the 'onion'.

Plate 11. VLADIMIR, Twelfth century

Church of St Dmitri. 1194–7. East end

Here is seen the beautiful eastern arcade, of which every third column runs right down to the ground. This is a special character of the Vladimir style.

Plate 12. VLADIMIR, Twelfth century

Church of St Dmitri. 1194–7. *Detail of south side*

Among the elaborate sculpturings on the upper parts of these walls are many subjects of west Asiatic origin, such as winged beasts and other monstrous creatures.

Plate 13. VLADIMIR, Twelfth century

Church of St Dmitri. 1194–7. Detail of west front

The complex pillars of the arcade are supported by corbels in the form of fantastic beasts. Within the arches are saints, standing above animal or vegetable subjects in very flat relief.

Plate 14. YURIEV POLSKI, Thirteenth century

1. *Sobor of St George. 1230–4. North side*

The entire surface of the walls of this church, other than the eastern, was originally covered with continuous sculptured designs. Unfortunately it has undergone extensive damage and alteration.

2. *The same. South-west corner*

This part of the building has been much tampered with at various periods. The medallions, containing saints' heads, were probably taken from another building now destroyed; they strikingly resemble those of a church at Akhtamar in Armenia, also those of Pthni (Pl. 99, 2).

PLATE 15. YURIEV POLSKI, Thirteenth century

2. *The same. Detail on north side of west porch*

Shows a type of diffuse carving in flat relief very unusual in Christian churches. The design consists of animal and vegetable forms, more or less conventionalised. Note the winged monsters and birds, which have a Persian origin.

1. *Sobor of St George. 1230–4. South porch*

At first sight strongly suggests a Romanesque doorway with Byzantinesque capitals. Somewhat similar work is found, however, in Armenia, with whose architecture the style of Vladimir may be more closely connected.

Plate 16. EARLY MOSCOW STYLE, Fourteenth century

1. *Zvenigorod. Sobor of the Assumption. Southern aspect*
Middle 14th cent.

One of the first churches to be built after the Mongol irruption of the thirteenth century, which had brought all building to a standstill

2. *The same. East end*

The arcade of the Vladimir style is here replaced by a band of carved ornament. The arcading of the apses is retained in a much simplified form

PLATE 17. EARLY MOSCOW STYLE, Fourteenth and Fifteenth centuries

2. *Sergievo. Sobor of the Trinity.* 1423

The monastery of Sergievo, founded about the same time that Moscow became the capital of Russia, was also a great centre of building activity. This, unlike the great Moscow cathedrals, was the work of native architects.

1. *Near Zvenigorod. Church of the Nativity of the Virgin in the Savino-Storozhevski Monastery*
End of 14th cent.

Similar to the last. An ornamental band encircles the whole church. The frescoes have been recently repainted, as have those of Sergievo in the next picture.

Plate 18. MOSCOW, Fifteenth century

Cathedral of the Assumption. 1475–9

The work of an Italian, who was instructed to reproduce the Cathedral of the Assumption at Vladimir (Pl. 9). This, the largest of the three cathedrals in the Kremlin at Moscow, was the coronation church of the Tsars (see Pl. 47 for the interior).

Plate 19. MOSCOW, Fifteenth century

Cathedral of the Annunciation. 1482–90

A smaller but very picturesque church, the work of architects from Pskov. Here there appear for the first time externally the 'encorbelled arches', later applied very widely in the Moscow style. The Tsars were married, and their children baptised, in this church.

Plate 20. MOSCOW, Sixteenth century

Cathedral of the Archangel Michael. 1505–9

Built, like the Assumption, by an Italian. Several features which appeared here for the first time found great popularity and were incorporated in the Russian style: notably the cornice, and the semi-circular spaces above it. This was the imperial burial place (see also Pl. 51, 2).

Plate 21. MOSCOW STYLE, Fifteenth to Sixteenth centuries

1. *Rostov Veliki. Cathedral of the Assumption*
15th–16th cent.

Shows the influence of the Cathedral of the Assumption at Moscow.

2. *Moscow. Sobor of the Novodevichi Monastery.* 1537

Built under the same influence. The remaining buildings of this monastery are all baroque (see Pl. 60).

3. *Sergievo. Church of the Presentation of the Virgin.* 1547

These two churches appear to be independent of the influence of the Kremlin cathedrals. In both, the east end bears the peculiar form of blind arcade seen here.

4. *Sergievo. Church of the Descent of the Holy Ghost.* 1559

Shows an ornamental band as in the older Cathedral of the Trinity close by; also ogee arches, very common in the sixteenth century.

Plate 22. MOSCOW, Sixteenth century. 'Tower' churches

1. *Dyakovo, near Moscow. Church of the Beheading of John the Baptist. 1529*

This type of church appeared as a novelty in the early part of the sixteenth century, owing to the influence of wooden architecture. This and the next church were undoubtedly prototypes of St Basil

2. *Kolomenskoe, near Moscow. Church of the Ascension. 1532*

Features of this church adopted directly from north-Russian wooden architecture are the great conical tower, the superposed arches, and the covered galleries and stairways round the base (compare the wooden church at Uga, Pl. 72, 2)

Plate 23. MOSCOW, Sixteenth century. 'Tower' church

1. *Ostrovo, near Moscow. Church of the Transfiguration. View from the east.* Middle 16th cent.

Like the former two churches, this one stands on high ground over-looking the valley of the Moskva River. It is another example of wooden influence.

2. *The same. North-western aspect*

In the decoration of this church much use is made of small arches of various forms (*kokoshniki*). In this view the lower part of the building is concealed by a growth of weeds and bushes.

Plate 24. MOSCOW, Sixteenth century

Church of St Basil. 1555–60. *View from west*

This famous building is not really typical of Russian architecture: as a whole it is an oddity, though all its individual features were used in many other buildings both before and after. The church consists of a central element around which are grouped eight almost separate tower-like chapels, four large, and four small.

Plate 25. MOSCOW, Sixteenth century

Church of St Basil. 1555–60. *Detail from south-east*

Some of the ornamental subjects (notably the flower-pots) are Italian. All the decoration, including the peculiar sculpturing of the domes, is picked out in a variety of bright colours. This colouring was, however, added in the seventeenth century; the same applies to the elaborate approaches to the building.

Plate 26. MOSCOW, Sixteenth century

Old Sobor in the Don Monastery. 1593. *View from north-east*

A type of church, peculiar to Moscow, in which *kokoshniki* assume great prominence; they are, however, purely decorative. Four of the five apses can be seen in this view; the lateral ones belong to side chapels.

Plate 27. MOSCOW, Sixteenth to Seventeenth centuries

1. *Moscow. St Irene*
16th cent.

An anomalous type with conical roof.
Now destroyed (?).

2. *Kazan. Bell tower in the Monastery of John the Baptist.* 16th cent.

Several bell towers of this form remain from the sixteenth century.

3. *Moscow. Church in the Monastery of the Nativity*

Second half of 16th cent.
With two rows of decorative *kokoshniki*, the upper ones alternating with the lower.

4. *Moscow. Church of the Intercession.* 1626.
View from north-west

Similar in all respects to the old cathedral in the Don Monastery, but with an extra row of small *kokoshniki* at the base of the cupola.

Plate 28. 'TENT' CHURCHES, Sixteenth to Seventeenth centuries

1. *Kazan. Church in the Monastery of John the Baptist.* 16th cent.

Three 'tents' raised on a single roof; they are probably merely ornamental.

2. *Uglich. Church of the Assumption in the Monastery of St Alexis.* 1628

This is one of the best examples of tent-roofed churches. Compare the wooden cathedral at Kem (Pl. 72).

3. *Nizhni Novgorod. Monastery of the Raising of the Cross.* 17th cent.?

A two-tented church. Below is seen the River Oká, crossed by the old bridge of boats (now replaced by a girder bridge). Beyond is the Volga, and on the tongue of land between the two rivers the grounds of the Nizhni Novgorod fair.

Plate 29. 'TENT' CHURCH, Seventeenth century

Moscow. Church of the Nativity of the Virgin. 1649–52

Much the most elaborate church of this class. A picturesque assemblage of tent-towers and *kokoshniki*, with the Italian cornice and semicircles, on an extremely irregular plan.

Plate 30. MOSCOW, Seventeenth century. Lesser Churches

1. *Church of the Assumption in Gonchari*

Shows the usual cornice and semi-circular spaces originating in the Italian Cathedral of the Archangel in the Kremlin.

2. *Church in the Monastery of the Miracle*

Eastern view. This prolongation of the east end in two stages is unusual.

3. *St Nicholas in Khamovniki*

A very ornate church with elaborate brick and tile work, and a row of *kokoshniki* round the edge of the roof. The low prolongation on the right joins the church to its bell tower.

4. *St Gregory of Neocaesarea.* **1679**

Shows the usual seventeenth-century combination of church and bell tower, the latter being connected by an extension on the western side of the church.

Plate 31. MOSCOW, Seventeenth century. Details

1. *Taininskoe, near Moscow. Church of the Annunciation.* Late 17th cent.

These symmetrical stairways indicate a relationship to north-Russian wooden architecture, as does the curved roof (*bochka*) between them.

2. *The same. Windows on south side*

Elaborate windows, often capped with much depressed ogee arches, are very common in the seventeenth century.

3. *The same. Detail of southern doorway*

Typical seventeenth-century brick work, unfortunately whitewashed over.

4. *Moscow. Porch and doorway of a seventeenth-century church*

One of the bottle-shaped pillars, usual in seventeenth-century porches, is seen here. The brick doorway resembles those of Yaroslavl.

Plate 32. MOSCOW, Seventeenth century

Church of the Georgian Virgin. 1653

One of the most pleasing of seventeenth-century churches in Moscow. The transition from the walls to the cupolas through several rows of *kokoshniki* is achieved with unusual success.

Plate 33. MOSCOW, Seventeenth century

Ostankino, near Moscow. Church of the Trinity. 1668

The most elaborate church in Moscow or its neighbourhood; the brick work is exceedingly complex. Ornament has here lost all connection with the structure of the building, while the dome-drums have reached an almost fantastic degree of attenuation.

Plate 34. YAROSLAVL, Seventeenth century

1. *Eastern view of a small church*
1 7th cent.

Many even of the lesser churches in Yaroslavl, of which this is a rather commonplace example, have side galleries crowned with extra domes.

2. *Church of the Epiphany*
Middle 17th cent.

Compare one of the Moscow churches (Pl. 30, 3). This building has, in addition, a cornice and the encircling gallery characteristic of Yaroslavl.

3. *Church of the Prophet Elias.* 1647

The earliest of the greater churches in Yaroslavl, with large galleries round the base. Of the two towers one is blind, and could not be used for bells. Compare one at Sergievo (Pl. 52, 1).

Plate 35. YAROSLAVL, Seventeenth century

Bell tower of St John Chrysostom. 1654

Probably the finest specimen of its type in the country. The very high, plain base is exceptional.

Plate 36. YAROSLAVL, Seventeenth century

St John Chrysostom. 1654. *North-west view*

Here the side chapels at the east end are crowned with 'tent' towers. Enormous porches, whose arches are provided with pen-

Plate 37. YAROSLAVL, Seventeenth century

St John the Baptist. 1687. *Southern porch*

Shows the elaborate panelled brick work which is a speciality of the architecture of Yaroslavl (see also Pl. 42, 1).

Plate 38. YAROSLAVL, Seventeenth century

St John the Baptist. 1687. *View from south*

The most striking of Yaroslavl churches. Of the fifteen brilliantly gilded domes, extra groups of five cover each of the two side chapels.

Plate 39. YAROSLAVL, Seventeenth century

1. *St John the Baptist.* 1687. *East end*

Showing five apses, of which the two outer belong to the side chapels.

2. *SS. Peter and Paul.* 1691. *East end*

One of the latest churches of Yaroslavl in this style. The chequered effect is due to paint, but the windows are surrounded by coloured faience (see Pl. 42, 2).

Plate 40. YAROSLAVL, Seventeenth century

St John the Baptist. 1687. *Western gallery and doorway into the church proper*

Characteristic seventeenth-century brick work in the door. This view is taken from inside the west porch, looking eastwards

Plate 41. YAROSLAVL, Seventeenth century

St John the Baptist. 1687. *Western gallery*

These galleries surround the Yaroslavl churches on all sides but the eastern. Vault and walls are alike smothered in highly coloured frescoes. These include many biblical and secular subjects borrowed from Dutch engravings, which were highly popular in Russia in the seventeenth century.

Plate 42. YAROSLAVL, Seventeenth century

2. *SS. Peter and Paul.* 1691. *Eastern window*

Formalised vegetable designs in faience form a frame for these windows. The rest of the decoration on the apses is painted.

1. *St John the Baptist.* 1687. *Detail of southern porch*

Wonderful variety is found in this brick work: among the small bosses alone about ten distinct designs are distinguishable in this photograph. A coloured tile forms the nucleus of each panel.

Plate 43. YAROSLAVL, Seventeenth century

2. *Approach to Church of St Nicholas*

A very charming adjunct to one of the Yaroslavl churches. It is richly decorated in brick panelling and coloured tiles.

1. *Entrance into church precincts of St John the Baptist.* 1687

A common form of gate, rising in three stages.

Plate 44. VOLGA TOWNS, Seventeenth century

1. *Romanovo Borisoglebsk (now called Tutaev). Sobor of the Ascension.* 1652–70

An enormous church, in a very small town. Notable for the double-storied gallery and its massive porches.

2. *The same. Gate in the surrounding wall*

Similar to one at Yaroslavl, but still larger, and taller in proportion.

3. *Uglich. St John the Baptist.* 1689–90

Not unlike some of the churches at Yaroslavl, but with broader galleries, and combined bell tower. The tower is built over the entrance way.

Plate 45. ROSTOV VELIKI, Seventeenth century

Church of St John Theologos. 1683. *East end*

Most of the churches in the Kremlin of Rostov the Great are actually built against its fortified wall, and pairs of towers (as seen here) are associated with each one. These churches are enormously tall, being built in two stories, and very thick walled, to resist attack.

Plate 46. VELIKI USTYUG, Seventeenth century

Church of the Ascension. 1648

The most striking building in a little town of many churches. The irregularity of the plan, and the profuse and varied ornament, showing a baroque tendency, give unusual picturesqueness to this church.

Plate 47. INTERIOR, Fifteenth century

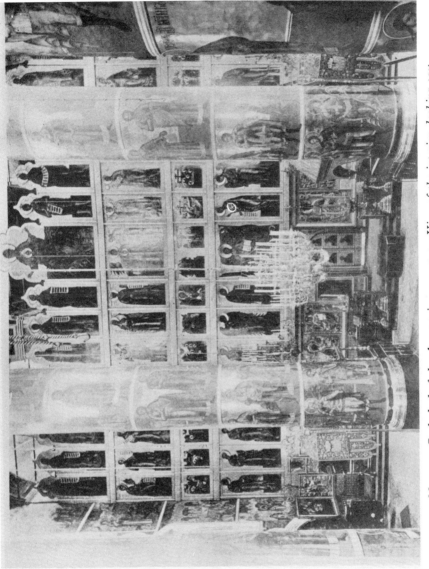

Moscow. Cathedral of the Assumption. 1475–9. View of the interior, looking east

This Italian-built cathedral has probably the most spacious interior of any church in Russia. The great round pillars are also noteworthy. The eastern pair are seen here, and parts of the western ones are just included at the sides of the picture. The five-storeyed *iconostas*, which is later than the church itself, is thickly encrusted with gold and precious stones. Note also the massive candelabra hanging in the position usual in all Russian churches (see Pl. 18 and the plan on p. 31).

Plate 48. INTERIOR, Seventeenth century

Yaroslavl. St Nicholas. View of the iconostas

A characteristic Russian interior showing the very tall and narrow proportions. On either side are seen the two square pillars of the western pair; the eastern pair are just behind the *iconostas* so that only their tops are visible. The central cupola is borne by these four principal pillars. In the middle of the *iconostas* is the elaborate 'royal door' through which only priests were allowed to pass.

Plate 49. INTERIOR, Seventeenth century

Yaroslavl. St Nicholas. View from the iconostas *looking south-westwards*

The south-western pillar and parts of the walls appear here, all covered with frescoes, as usual in the churches of Yaroslavl. In the foreground is the canopied 'Tsar's place' where the Tsar would have sat when he attended service here. A corresponding throne for the Patriarch was located opposite, on the north side of the church. On the right is an icon before which a lamp hangs.

Plate 50. MOSCOW, Sixteenth and Seventeenth centuries. Civil Architecture

1. *The Iberian Gate (sixteenth century?) and Chapel of the Iberian Virgin (1669)*

The chapel contained one of the most venerated pictures of the Virgin in all Russia. It was removed in 1928, and the gate itself subsequently demolished to facilitate traffic to and from the Red Square.

2. *The Spaski Gate (Gate of the Redeemer) into the Kremlin. 1625*

An interesting addition to the many foreign buildings of the Moscow Kremlin. This tower, Gothic in style, was built by an English clock-maker named Christopher Galloway.

Plate 51. MOSCOW, Sixteenth and Seventeenth centuries. The Kremlin

2. *Tower of Ivan Veliki. 1600. Also Cathedral of the Archangel Michael. 1505–9*

A view from outside the Kremlin wall, part of which appears in the picture. The Archangel Cathedral, being much nearer, here looks disproportionately tall (see Pl. 20).

1. *Bell tower of Ivan Veliki (John the Great) and two other belfries in the Kremlin*

The great tower, 320 ft. high, dominates the whole Kremlin. It was completed by Boris Godunov in 1600. The two smaller belfries adjoining were built later. Below them is the gigantic 'tsar bell'.

Plate 52. TOWERS, Sixteenth to Seventeenth centuries

1. *Sergievo. Tower of the Church of SS. Zossima and Sabbatius.* 1635-7

An almost windowless type unsuitable for bells. Probably also a primitive form: it closely resembles the 'tents' of wooden churches (see Pl.68).

2. *Sergievo. Church of St Pyatnitsa.* 1547

An early bell tower with open arches below the conical roof; the latter also has four simple openings.

3. *Kolomenskoe, near Moscow. Gate.* 1652-73

An open tower in which the 'tent' remains unpierced. Both these towers of Kolomenskoe are built over arches.

4. *Kolomenskoe, near Moscow. Entrance to Church of Our Lady of Kazan*

Similar to the tower illustrated above in its upper parts, but with eight openings in the roof instead of four.

Plate 53. BELL TOWERS, Seventeenth century

1. *Moscow. St Demetrius of Salonica. Bell tower*

Unusual in that the whole tower is four-sided, and the roof pyramidal rather than conical.

2. *Near Zvenigorod. Belfry of the Savino-Storozhevski Monastery*

Another exceptional belfry culminating in three separate 'tent' towers.

3. *Nizhni Novgorod. Bell tower*

These two specimens illustrate the two extremes of elaboration found in this type of belfry. Here there is but a single row of windows in the roof. Two or three tiers are very common (see for instance Pls. 34 and 44).

4. *Moscow. St Nicholas*

No less than four tiers of windows, the lowest series being double, and many other elaborations. This fine tower, which stood in the Arbat at Moscow, has unfortunately been pulled down.

Plate 54. BELL TOWERS, Seventeenth century

1. *Pskov. Tower*
16th–17th cent.?

Here a not very pleasing cupola replaces the usual conical roof. None of the lines in this building are perpendicular.

2. *Moscow. Church of the Assumption in Pechatniki.* 17th cent.

A somewhat anomalous tower in which the usual form has been duplicated.

3. *Kazan. Tower*
17th cent.?

This pair of towers illustrates a distinct type, in which the cone or 'tent' has been abandoned. Here there are two storeys in which bells could be hung.

4. *Yaroslavl. Tower*
17th cent.?

A four-storeyed tower. Another similar one, but much more elaborate, adjoins St John the Baptist at Yaroslavl.

Plate 55. DEFENSIVE TOWERS, Sixteenth to Seventeenth centuries

1. *Moscow. Tower in wall of Kitai Gorod.* 1534–8

This wall, with many towers of similar form, encircled the inner city of Moscow, lying east of the Kremlin.

2. *Moscow. Tower in the fortified wall of the Simonov Monastery.* 16th cent.?

An unusually massive round corner tower. This and other monasteries to the south of Moscow formed the outer defences of the capital.

3. *Kazan. Sumbeka tower*
16th–17th cent.

Generally said to be a Tartar rather than a Russian building, though the contrary has been claimed. It is a most graceful addition to the Kremlin of Kazan.

4. *Moscow. South-west corner of the Kremlin wall. Towers of seventeenth century*

The tower on the right is virtually a copy of the Sumbeka tower at Kazan. It rises over the Borovitski Gate, through which Napoleon entered the Kremlin in 1812.

Plate 56. UKRAINIAN WOOD, Seventeenth to Eighteenth centuries

1. *Kiev. St John the Baptist*
End of 17th cent.

Showing the common arrangement of three elements in a straight line, apart from the belfry. No longer exists.

2. *Velika Berezyanka (province of Kiev)*
18th cent.

Five elements are arranged in the form of a cross: each has its own cupola. Compare fig. 1 on the opposite page.

3. *Lyulintsi (province of Kiev). Bell tower*
End of 17th or beginning of 18th cent.

A little belfry rising in two stages. Many Ukrainian belfries are much more elaborate. (Long since destroyed.)

4. *Village Church in Galicia*
18th cent.?

Five-fold and cruciform like the church above, but these Galician examples are of squatter proportions and the eaves are more prominent.

Plate 57. UKRAINIAN BAROQUE, Seventeenth century

1. *Kiev. Church "at the trading gates" in the Lavra*

Shows the influence of a common form of Ukrainian wooden church (see fig. 2 opposite).

2. *Kiev. Church of the Assumption in the Lavra*

Note the pilasters, the highly ornamented window frames, and the deformed pediment which crowns the façade; features all typically baroque.

3. *Kiev. General view of the Cathedral of St Sophia from south-east.* 1036
17th cent. additions.

The ancient St Sophia, of which the five apses are alone visible here, forms merely the nucleus of this enormous pile, whose outer aspect is due almost entirely to additions in the Ukrainian baroque style (see also Pl. 1).

Plate 58. MOSCOW BAROQUE, Seventeenth century

2. *Church of the Assumption in Pokrovki.* 1696—9

Almost as original in plan as the church at Fili. This building is
said to have excited the admiration of Napoleon, who took
steps to prevent its destruction in the conflagration of 1812.

1. *St Nicholas "of the Great Cross"*
End of 17th cent.

In this church the traditional Russian square form with five
domes is preserved; but the detail is thoroughly baroque.

2.   *Sukharev Tower.* 1692–1701

One of the most conspicuous landmarks in Moscow. From a gigantic square base rises an octagonal tower on more traditional lines. It was built by Peter the Great.

1.   *Fili, near Moscow. Church of the Intercession.* 1693

The form of this remarkable church, rising in several stages, shows the influence of Ukrainian wooden architecture. An open gallery surrounds the four-lobed base of the building, and from it radiate four immense stairways, each dividing into two flights below.

Plate 60. MOSCOW BAROQUE, Seventeenth century

I. *Novodevichi Monastery. Tower in the wall*

These towers are decidedly ornamental rather than
defensive. Both are built over gateways.

2. *The same. Another tower*

The storeyed arrangement takes after certain types
of wooden churches in the Ukraine.

**3. *The same. The great Bell tower of the
Monastery.* 1688**

Note the elaborated window-frames, cornices and
balustrades characteristic of the baroque style every-
where. Compare the 'storeyed' towers in Pl. 54.

**4. *The same. Church of the Intercession
on the Monastery wall***

Three elements are arranged along the east-west
axis, as in a common type of Ukrainian wooden
church.

Plate 61. MOSCOW BAROQUE, Seventeenth to Eighteenth centuries

1. *Moscow. Church of Our Lady of Vladimir.* 1691–4

This again reproduces a single-domed Ukrainian type. Behind is one of the towers in the wall of the Kitai Gorod.

2. *Moscow. St Nikita the Martyr*
17th cent.

Similar, but a large belfry is connected to the church on the west side.

3. *Moscow. Church of the Praise of Our Lady.* 1705

An attractive little church following pre-baroque tradition in general plan and the arrangement of its domes. Now destroyed.

4. *Nizhni Novgorod. Church of the Most Holy Virgin.* 1719

Here the domes are arranged on the axes of the church, not on the diagonals. This is one of the most richly ornamented of provincial churches in the baroque style.

Plate 62. LATE BAROQUE ARCHITECTURE

Uglich. Church of the Nativity. 1801

A very late church, illustrating the survival of a more or less Russian tradition into a period characterised by pseudo-classical architecture. The church itself shows the domes arranged on the axes, a plan which, originating in the Ukraine, became very popular during the baroque period. The tower is a very pleasing example; this type, with tapering *flèche* derived from western Europe, did not appear in Russia until the eighteenth century.

Plate 63. DOMESTIC ARCHITECTURE

Remains of domestic architecture of this period are exceedingly scarce. This is an attractive little red brick building. The quite convincing covered stairway was added in the course of a restoration in 1892.

1. *Uglich. Palace of the Tsarevich Dmitri.* 1481

2. *Moscow. Boyar House*
17th cent.

Although the original building was too ruinous to be closely reproduced, this restoration probably gives a good idea of the house of a Russian Boyar (noble) in the seventeenth century.

Plate 64. MOSCOW

1. *Moscow. General view of the Kremlin*

In the centre rises the great belfry of Ivan Veliki. To its left stand, in order, the Cathedrals of the Assumption (partly hidden), the Archangel Michael (standing up conspicuously) and the Annunciation (against the wall of the Great Palace). To the right of the belfries appears a canopy which covered a memorial to Alexander II; the whole monument was removed in 1928 (see also Pls. 18–20; 51).

2. *Moscow. Continuation of the same view to the left*

The Kremlin wall is seen continued as far as the 'water tower' at the south-west corner. In the distance is seen the gigantic modern Cathedral of the Redeemer, built to commemorate the final worsting of Napoleon in 1812. It was destroyed in 1931 (see also Pl. 55, 4).

Plate 65. SERGIEVO AND KOSTROMA

1. *Sergievo. General view of the Troitsko-Sergievskaya Lavra (Trinity Monastery of St Sergius)*

In the centre is the Cathedral of the Assumption; this and the walls are of the sixteenth century. To the left of the cathedral is the seventeenth-century refectory, and behind it a tall belfry by Rastrelli, who carried on the baroque tradition during the eighteenth century.

2. *Kostroma, seen from the Volga*

One of the upper Volga towns with much of architectural interest, but second in this respect to Yaroslavl and Uglich. Within the Kremlin wall are seen a seventeenth-century cathedral and an eighteenth-century belfry.

Plate 66. WOODEN ARCHITECTURE. Elementary forms

1. Izba (peasant's dwelling) at Kizhi on Lake Onega

A modern *izba*, but retaining the primitive rectangular form of the earliest wooden structures. The outside stairway and covered platform (*kryltso*), originating in these domestic buildings, was adopted and much elaborated in wooden church architecture.

2. Octagonal chapel at Belaya Sluda, near the Northern Dvina River
17th cent.

The most primitive possible form of eight-sided chapel, from which the high 'tent-roofed' octagon was probably derived. The octagon was used exclusively in ecclesiastical buildings. The cross is missing here.

Plate 67. RECTANGULAR CHURCHES

1. Near Kizhi. Simple rectangular chapel

Late in date but very early in type. An elementary *kryltso* at the west end leads to two simple rectangular spaces. The flattening of the logs outside, and covering of the corners with upright boards, are recent innovations detracting much from the charm of these wooden buildings.

2. Chukhcherma, near Archangel. Rectangular church
17th cent.

A pleasing and characteristic example of rectangular church with 'wedge-shaped' roof. As usual in wooden churches, there are three compartments; here, however, the first division is exceptionally long and there is a break in its roof. The *kryltso* has a double stairway leading to a common platform.

Plate 68. OCTAGONAL 'TENT' CHURCH

Belaya Sluda. Church of Our Lady of Vladimir. 1642. View from west

A magnificent example of one of the oldest types of wooden church on octagonal plan. It is about 150 ft. high. Originally the roof was covered with shingles, but these have been replaced by over-lapping boards, except at the tip of the conical 'tent' roof. The same system of construction by means of horizontal timbers, as seen in the walls, is carried on to the very top of the cone; there are no uprights.

Plate 69. OCTAGONAL 'TENT' CHURCH

1. *Belaya Sluda. Church of Our Lady of Vladimir. 1642. North-east view*

Showing the projection from the eastern face of the octagon, forming the sanctuary, with the altar.

2. *The same. View from south*

Shows the symmetrical extensions of the church to east and west. At the western end is a form of *kryltso*, which is approached through open galleries on the north and south sides of the building. A stairway leading to this gallery is seen here.

Plate 70. RECTANGULAR 'TENT' CHURCH

Kondopoga, on Lake Onega. Church of the Assumption, and bell tower. 1774

This church, and its bell tower on the left, show a combination of the rectangular and octagonal types: in each case the plan is square, but a transition to the octagon is effected above. The unusual and highly picturesque disposition of the stairways approach at

PLATE II. RECTANGULAR 'TENT' CHURCHES

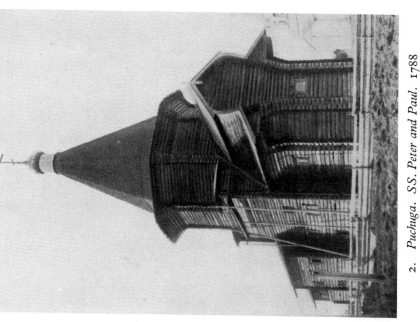

1. *Kondopoga. Church of the Assumption.* 1774

Showing the great height and the narrowness of this church, giving a very remarkable silhouette.

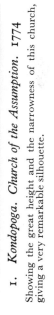

2. *Puchuga. SS. Peter and Paul.* 1788

Though even later in date, this church, with its more normal proportions, probably represents a much older type than the example on the left.

Plate 72. MULTIPLE 'TENT' CHURCH

1. Kem, on the White Sea. Sobor of the Assumption. 1714.
Eastern view

Consists of three almost separate elements of the type illustrated on
The whole building is somewhat spoilt by modern

2. The same, before "restoration".
Western elevation

A rather idealised drawing, as the lines cannot have been strictly
vertical when it was made. The round timbers, interlocking at the
in their original state; also the little arches

2. *Una, on the White Sea. St Clement*
17th cent.

The arches (*bochki*) applied to the central element of the church are here seen in two tiers. This type is an early one, and had an important influence on brick architecture of the Moscow period (see Pl. 22, 2).

1. *Berezovets on the Nola (province of Kostroma). St Nicholas*
18th cent.

In these cruciform churches the central element is extended in all four directions, not to east and west only. Here the usual 'tent' roof is replaced by a group of cupolas. A fine gallery surrounds the church.

Plate 74. 'ALEMBIC-ROOFED' CHURCHES

1. *Podporozhie, near Onega, on the White Sea. Church of the Trinity.* 1725–7

Churches with this peculiar form of roof are especially frequent in the neighbourhood of Onega. For the adjoining bell tower see Pl. 81, 4.

2. *Podporozhie. Church of Our Lady of Vladimir.* 1745

This has a cruciform plan. Each projection carries a 'tent' crowned by a dome; the whole complement of domes gives the general outline of a cone.

3. *Podporozhie. Church of the Trinity.* 1725–7

A smaller chapel is built against the side of the principal church; its roof and dome make an important contribution to the general effect.

Plate 75. 'MANY-DOMED' AND 'STOREYED' CHURCHES

1. *Kizhi, on Lake Onega. Church of the Intercession.* Early 18th cent.

Originally these nine-domed churches had a square central element on which five domes were arranged as in brick architecture, and one more was added in the centre of each side. Here the square passes into an octagon, and the central dome is surrounded by eight others in a circle.

2. *Belaya Sluda, near the Northern Dvina. St Athanasius.* 1753

This 'storeyed' variety of wooden church probably originated in the Ukraine, where it is the usual type (see Pl. 56).

Plate 76. CHURCH OF KIZHI

Kizhi. Church of the Transfiguration. From south-east
Early 18th cent.

The most elaborate and arresting creation of north-Russian wooden architecture. Its plan is an octagon converted into a cross by projections on alternate sides. Above these arms of the cross are the principal flights of domes. Although always described as having 21, the church has in fact 22 domes, as an inspection of these photographs will show.

Plate 77. CHURCH OF KIZHI

1. *Church of the Transfiguration. From east.* Early 18th cent.

The churches of Kizhi form a wonderfully picturesque group on one of the islands in the middle of Lake Onega. Besides the two buildings seen here, the Church of the Intercession (Pl. 75, 1) stands adjacent.

2. *The same. Western approach*

A massive *kryltso*, with double stairway and elaborate carved balustrades leads to the western door of the church.

Plate 78. LESSER WOODEN CHURCHES AND CHAPELS

2. *Small church near Kizhi, on Lake Onega*
18th–19th cent.?

An extremely simple and attractive little church. The bell tower is simply perched on the roof at the west end.

1. *Village church of Zalyoskaya, near Chukhcherma, on the Northern Dvina*

Churches and their bell towers were never combined until the very end of the seventeenth century. This specimen was very possibly built during the eighteenth.

3. *Chapel at Medvedevskaya, near Onega, on the White Sea*

Both these diminutive chapels are asymmetrical in plan. Here a little cone or 'tent' is combined with the steeply sloping roof.

4. *Chapel at Amosovskaya, near Onega*

Another 'tented' chapel. The little porch (*kryltso*) is on the north side.

Plate 79. CHURCH WITH COMBINED BELL TOWER

Kem, on the White Sea. Small wooden church

One of two wooden churches in the town of Kem (see also Pl. 72). The combined bell tower, and the rather squat proportions, suggesting degeneracy, show that this is a very late example. A large modern brick church appears in the background.

Plate 80. WOODEN BELL TOWER

Tsivozero, near the Northern Dvina. Small bell tower. 1658

A very small and delightful example, probably of the most ancient type, such as appeared in north Russia about the fifteenth century. The church which it accompanied has vanished.

Plate 81. WOODEN BELL TOWERS

1. *Tsivozero. Tower of 1658*

The plan is octagonal, no doubt the original condition. In this and the next tower two different methods of jointing the logs at the corners are exemplified.

**2. *Chukhcherma, near Archangel.
Tower of 1657***

In this contemporary example an innovation is seen: the base of the tower is square, though it passes quickly into the octagon.

**3. *Kizhi, on Lake Onega. Bell tower*
Early 18th cent.**

A later tower in which the square base has assumed much greater prominence.

**4. *Podporozhie, near Onega.
Bell tower of 1725–7***

Here the usual conical roof is replaced by a low dome bearing a spike or *flèche*. This feature is not met with before the eighteenth century.

Plate 82. CENTRALISED CHURCH, Sixth to Seventh centuries

1. *Mtskhet (Georgia). Djuari church. South-east view*

This ancient church, like many others in Georgia, is built on the brink of a precipice. From here one may see a fine view of Mtskhet, the capital of Georgia before Tiflis (see Pl. 101, 2).

2. *The same. View from north-east*

In these centralised churches the dome is relatively very large, and not supported by internal columns. Its thrust is taken by 'apse-buttresses', one of which is here seen projecting in the middle of each side, flanked by recesses.

1. *Echmiadzin (Armenia). St Ripsima.* 7th cent.

An Armenian centralised church. The dome is very large (46 ft. across). Here the 'apse-buttresses' do not project but their position is marked by pairs of deep recesses in the walls. The porch dates from the seventeenth, and the bell turret above it from the eighteenth century.

2. *Sion (Georgia). Basilican church.* 7th or 8th cent.?

This entirely different and intrusive type of church existed alongside the native centralised buildings from about the fifth to the eighth century. Originating in Mesopotamia, it was introduced into Armenia and Georgia from Syria.

Plate 84. ARMENIA, Tenth to Thirteenth centuries

Sanaïn. General view of the Monastery from south-west

This and the neighbouring monastery of Haghpat are situated in wild mountainous country between Tiflis and Leninakan (Alex-andropol). This almost impregnable area was a stronghold of Armenian culture during the middle ages. The larger church here is the earliest of the group; its entrance hall at the west end dates from the twelfth, and the bell tower from the thirteenth century. Compare the finer specimen in Pl. 161.

Plate 85. ARMENIA, Tenth or Eleventh centuries

1. *Sanaïn. Church of the Saviour. 1048-65?*

Eastern aspect of the larger church seen in the general view above. The characteristic arcading and window are very early examples of this style of decoration though there seems to be some doubt whether this (and the next) church were built in the tenth or eleventh century.

2. *Haghpat. Principal church of the Monastery*
10th or 11th cent.

Characteristic recesses are seen here on the south and east faces of the building. Note also the carving in the eastern gable, representing the Kings Sumbat and Kvirik II, the builders of the church, holding a little model of it in their hands.

Plate 86. ARMENIA, Tenth to Thirteenth centuries

2. *Haghpat. Entrance hall to the church*
13th cent.?

The ornamental band shows very typical Armenian decoration. It is strictly geometrical, and the component strands of the design cross each other only at right angles.

1. *Sanain. Church of the Saviour. Arcading at north-east corner.* 10th or 11th cent.

These double or triple semi-columns are not made up of independent stones but are cut in the general surface. Note the carved capitals, reminiscent of Assyrian work, the irregular spacing of the columns, and the curious boast at the lower left-hand corner.

Plate 87. ARMENIA, Thirteenth century

2. *Haghpat. Small chapel in the Monastery*
13th cent.?

Here the drum is provided only with four simple windows. The
type of door seen in both these chapels has its counterpart in
many Mahommedan buildings.

1. *Haghpat. Small chapel above the village*
(Date?)

The drum has a delicate blind arcade with trefoil arches derived
from Mahommedan sources.

Plate 88. ARMENIAN DETAILS

1. *Kehardt. South doorway of church*
13th cent.

These two doors show characteristic Armenian geometrical carving.

2. *Haghpat. Western door of entrance hall*
13th cent.

An enormously elaborated arch surrounds a comparatively small door.

3. *Haghpat. Door of a subsidiary building*
13th cent.

An ogee arch in two orders: suggests Mahommedan influence. The stonework immediately above the door has the structure of a true arch.

4. *Sanaïn. Door of a small chapel*
12th cent.

An early pointed arch. The stepped form given to the ornamental pediment over this doorway is common in Armenia.

Plate 89. ARMENIAN DETAILS

1. *Kehardt. Doorway of a church*
13th cent.

A kink in the mouldings here takes the place of a capital. Compare the two lower figures on previous page.

2. *Pthni (Bethany). Archivolt in a ruined church*
7th cent.

An extremely early specimen of an elaborately carved archivolt. See details on next page.

3. *Pthni. Inner view of a ruinous church*
7th cent.

Showing the remains of a 'squinch' bridging the angle between the two arches diverging from the top of the pier on the left. Compare Pl. 104.

4. *The same, showing compound pier*

These compound piers show a parallelism with those developed during the Romanesque-Gothic transition centuries later. Note the spiral ornament on the capitals.

Plate 90. ARMENIAN FIGURE SCULPTURE

1. *Sevan, on Lake Gokcha. Part of a cross-slab*
(Date?)

It is unusual to find so much figure sculpture on these stones. The central figure, with upraised arms, follows a type of Asiatic derivation rather common in Armenia.

2. *Pthni, near Erivan. Detail of archivolt*
7th cent.

These medallions may be compared with those at Yuriev Polski in Russia (Pl. 14, 2). The form of the bird below shows the influence of a circular frame, though this has been lost.

3. *The same. Springing of archivolt*

A mounted warrior with bow and arrow attacking a dragon of some kind. Wonderfully spirited sculpture for so early a date.

4. *The same. Springing of archivolt*

Spearman attacking a lion. Both these are typical Sassanian (Persian) subjects: these later became popular throughout the Byzantine world, and in the West.

Plate 91. ARMENIAN HACHKAR (Memorial stone)

Stone at Haghpat
12th cent.?

These marvellous stones are extremely abundant in Armenia. They stand erect, like the Celtic cross-slabs of Scotland, but unlike these are carved on one side only. The Armenian sculptors cared nothing for exact symmetry, and studiously avoided re-duplicating their designs: even in a series of such stones one fails to find a single pattern repeated.

Plate 92. GEORGIA, Eleventh or Twelfth century (?)

1. *Kazbek. Church of Tsminda Sameba*
10th–12th cent.

There can be few churches in the world so wonderfully placed as this one. It stands on the very top of a steep hill just below the immense white peak of Mount Kazbek. The church was fortified, and no doubt used as a place of refuge.

2. *Kazbek. Distant view of the same church; an ancient guard-tower on the left*

The church is seen perched high up on the right. It overlooks the Georgian Military road between Tiflis and Vladikavkaz some miles to the north of the watershed, and lies therefore outside Transcaucasia proper.

Plate 93. GEORGIA, Eleventh or Twelfth century (?)

1. *Kazbek. Tsminda Sameba. Upper part of church from north-west*

The plan is a simple square and the walls are flat, without recesses. A slit-like window forms the nucleus of a design spreading widely over the wall. The nature of the stone work is well seen here: it forms the facing over a core of rubble-concrete which is seen exposed on part of the transept to the left.

The arch and the jambs of this doorway are cut in single pieces of stone. A very common geometrical design runs right round the door; the sculptured bosses and medallions, and the cross on the wall above, are likewise very characteristic of Georgian, as distinct from Armenian architecture.

2.   *The same. Western doorway*

Plate 94. GEORGIA, Eleventh century

Mtskhet. East end of the Cathedral.

The cathedral of Mtskhet is remarkable for its relatively enormous size. Outside it is distinguished by the free use of ornamental arcading, with multiple semi-columns. At the east end are two recesses marking the position of three internal apses, and each recess is included within an arch of appropriate height.

Plate 95. GEORGIA, Eleventh century

1. *Mtskhet. South-western view of the Cathedral.* 11th cent.

Showing another unique peculiarity of this cathedral: the transept roof is interrupted, just as is that of the main body of the church. It is as if two basilicas (of the type seen in Pl. 83, 2) were made to intersect at right angles. The two extensions at the west end of the building are also unusual.

2. *Gelati. South side of the principal church.* End of 11th cent.

Shows the usual type of transept with simple roof. Various non-constructional or 'atectonic' features are seen here, such as the arches which are made to turn round the corners of the transept.

Plate 96. GEORGIA, Eleventh to Twelfth centuries

Gelati (near Kutaïs). Principal church of the Monastery. East end
End of 11th and beginning of 12th cent.

One of the most dignified churches in Georgia. It shows the uncommon character of freely projecting apses at the eastern end; the central one of these has very beautiful blind arcading (see also Pls. 95, 2; 98; 99; 103).

Plate 97. GEORGIA, Twelfth century

Mtskhet. Church of the Samtavro Monastery. East end

As in the cathedral of Mtskhet, which this church resembles in many ways, the apses do not project, but the spaces between them are marked by recesses. (Contrast the photograph opposite.) The very rich ornamentation on the drum and the ends of the transepts show the somewhat later date of this building.

Plate 98. GEORGIA, Eleventh to Twelfth centuries

Gelati. South-west view of the principal church
End of 11th and beginning of 12th cent.

Showing the very satisfying proportions of this church: compare the view from the opposite stand-point on Pl. 96. All the buildings in this monastery gain much from the beautiful expanse of closely cropped grass on which they stand.

Plate 99. GEORGIA, Eleventh to Twelfth centuries

Gelati. Detail of the principal church; chapel of twelfth century (?) beyond

Many characters separate this round-headed arcading from superficially similar Romanesque work in western Europe. The columns and arches are not made up of separate pieces, but are simply moulded in large blocks forming part of the facing of the wall. In the columns themselves, no distinction is made between base and capital, and both these are here left plain, while the shafts receive sculpturings at their ends.

Plate 100. GEORGIA, Sixteenth or Seventeenth century, and modern

1. *Ananur. A fortress with churches*
16th–17th cent.

It overlooks the Georgian Military Road about 40 miles north of Tiflis. The church shows little change of style since the twelfth century; the roof, however, is steepened and heightened.

2. *Ananur. Principal church*
16th–17th cent.

The southern façade seen here has a huge cross, which has now lost all connection with the windows; it is flanked by two trees standing above figures of saints.

3. *Tiflis. Modern church*

Showing a still greater degree of attenuation, by which character alone are the modern churches of Transcaucasia clearly distinguished from the mediaeval ones.

Plate 101. GEORGIA

1.   Gelati.   View of the Monastery

A splendid site among the foothills of the Caucasus, whose high snow peaks can be seen in the distance. The individual buildings, numbering two churches, a bell tower and a small chapel over a well, are shown on Pls. 95–6; 98–9; 102–3; 105, 2.

2.   Mtskhet.   View of the old capital from the Djuari church

Mtskhet was capital of Georgia before the sixth century. In the middle rises the huge cathedral (Pls. 94–5) and on the extreme right the Samtavro Monastery (Pls. 97; 105). The site is at the junction of the Rivers Kura and Aragva; they are now flooded owing to the building of a power station below. This view is from near the ancient Djuari church (Pl. 82).

Plate 102. GEORGIAN DETAILS

1. *Gelati. Chapel over a well*
About 12th cent.?

Round arches and a pointed one are here seen together. A stairway leads up to the tiny chapel on top.'

2. *Kazbek. Window in the Tsminda Sameba bell tower*

A delightful instance of neglected symmetry. The identity or signification of the beasts is entirely obscure.

3. *Gelati. Window of smaller church*
12th cent.?

An interlaced design is used very similar to that seen in the Kazbek doorway (Pl. 93, 2).

4. *The same. Another window (blocked up)*
12th cent.?

With two very simple geometrical figures based on interlocked polygons.

Plate 103. GEORGIAN DETAILS

Gelati. North door of the principal church
End of 11th cent.

This interlaced zig-zag design combined with a leaf-like 'palmette' is extremely common in Georgia, though not in Armenia. Note the discontinuity of the lines between some of the adjacent blocks of stone, showing that these were not carved *in situ*. The peculiar columns on each side of the door, with their square capitals and square bases, resemble those of the arcade on the south side of the church (Pl. 99); but they support nothing.

Plate 104. ARMENIAN BELL TOWER

Haghpat. Bell tower in the Monastery
13th cent.

A form of bell tower peculiar to Armenia. In this example the corners are curiously recessed. The recesses are covered above by 'squinch' arches, structures usually used internally for bridging the corners of a square (Pl. 89, 3). The upper part of the base is thus eight-sided. The spirelet containing the bells is supported on seven pillars.

Plate 105. GEORGIAN BELL TOWERS

1. *Kazbek. Tower adjoining the church of Tsminda Sameba.* 12th cent.?

Compare Pls. 92–3; 102, 2. A square base is surmounted by an open spirelet of octagonal form.

2. *Gelati. Bell tower in the Monastery* About 12th cent.?

Of the same general form, with differences in detail, and more elaboration in the open arches.

3. *Mtskhet. Bell tower of the Samtavro Monastery.* 15th or 16th cent.?

In this much later specimen the square base is taller and itself pierced, while there are twelve openings above.

4. *Tiflis. Isolated bell tower.* 18th cent.

Showing the persistence of the same tradition into modern times. The material, however, is brick, which was scarcely used in the mediaeval architecture of Transcaucasia.

Plate 106. RUMANIA, Sixteenth century

1. *Curtea de Arges. The Cathedral. 1517. South-west view*

This remarkable church, undoubtedly the finest in Rumania, holds an almost isolated position in the architectural world. It is included here as an example of Armenian or Georgian influence in the Balkans.

2. *The same from south-east*

A rare achievement by the architect of this building was his grouping of the cupolas, which are so disposed that they combine well from whatever angle viewed. One regrets, however, the twisted form of the western pair.

Plate 107. RUMANIA, Sixteenth century

1. *Curtea de Argeş. The Cathedral. 1517.*
    Doorway at the west end

The only entrance to the church. It has much in common with some Mahommedan doorways, and may be compared also with the Armenian ones shown on Pls. 87 and 88, 1. The elaborate cusping of the arch has exact parallels in Armenia as well as the Mahommedan countries.

2. *The same. Detail of the south side*

The principal character borrowed from Transcaucasia is the external blank-arcading. This differs, however, from the usual Armenian form in being divided into two tiers, of which the lower here takes the form of a series of panels. In this and other Rumanian churches a great twisted cable, completely surrounding the building, separates the two arcades.

Plate 108. RUMANIA, Sixteenth century

1. Curtea de Argeş. The Cathedral. 1517. View from the east

Showing its unusually narrow and tall proportions, mainly due to the raising of each cupola on a square base.

2. The same. View of western quadrangle and fountain

Such a court, with a fountain in the middle, would be expected before a mosque, but is a most unusual addition to a Christian church. The cusped arches of the canopy resemble that of the doorway opposite.

BIBLIOGRAPHY

INDEX

RECENT BIBLIOGRAPHY

RUSSIA

In Russian

Игорь Грабарь. Исторія Русскаго Искусства. (IGOR GRABAR (Editor). *History of Russian Art.*) Moscow, from 1909. The standard work on Russian Art in general, excellently produced and illustrated. The first two volumes deal with the subject matter of this book (excluding Transcaucasia).

Викторъ Никольскій. Исторія Русскаго Искусства. (VIKTOR NIKOLSKI. *History of Russian Art.*) Moscow, 1915. The first volume deals shortly with all branches of Russian art up to the eighteenth century. A second volume on the modern period was never published. Some good illustrations, including coloured plates.

Мих. Красовскій. Очеркъ Исторіи Московскаго Періода Древне-русскаго Церковнаго Зодчества. (M. KRASOVSKI. *Sketch of the History of Old-Russian Church Architecture of the Moscow Period.*) Moscow, 1911. A very detailed monograph on the buildings of this period, but restricted to those of Moscow itself and the surrounding country.

Мих. Красовскій. Курсъ Исторіи Русской Архитектуры. Часть 1. Деревянное Зодчество. (M. KRASOVSKI. *Course* [of instruction] *in the History of Russian Architecture. Part 1. Wooden Architecture.*) Petrograd, 1916. A detailed and profusely illustrated account of northern and Ukrainian wooden architecture, domestic and ecclesiastical. The second volume, which would have dealt with stone and brick building, is unpublished.

Шмидт. Искусство Древней Руси Украйны. (SCHMIDT. *Art of the Ancient Ukraine.*) Kharkov, 1919. Concerns the architecture of the Kiev period, and its origins.

Иван Евдокимов. Север в Истории Русского Искусства. (IVAN EVDOKIMOV. *The North in the History of Russian Art.*) Vologda, 1920. Contains a long and interesting chapter on the North-Russian wooden style, written by an enthusiast. The illustrations are useless.

А. И. Некрасов. Византийское и Русское Искусство. (A. I. NEKRASOV. *Byzantine and Russian Art.*) Moscow, 1924. A small and very useful book with a good collection of diagrams, intended for the use of students. Deals almost exclusively with architecture.

A number of books on individual towns are omitted here.

In German

M. ALPATOV und N. BRUNOV. *Geschichte der Altrussischen Kunst.* Dr Benno Filser, Augsburg, 1932. A large volume of text and a thinner volume of plates, many of which are new. Architecture is dealt with by Brunov, painting and sculpture by Alpatov. In this book the importance of northern wooden architecture is minimised and its influence on brick almost denied.

Fanina Hallé. *Altrussische Kunst*. Berlin, 1920; Paris (Crès), 1922.

G. K. Lukomski. *Altrussische Kunst*. München, 1924.

Alexander Eliasberg. *Russische Baukunst*. Georg Müller, München, 1922. A short introduction precedes a quite good set of plates in half-tone, nearly all reproduced from Grabar. They cover both the ancient and the modern periods of Russian architecture.

In French

Louis Réau. *L'Art Russe, des Origines à Pierre le Grand*. Laurens, Paris, 1921. An admirable and inexpensive book; by far the best general account of Russian architecture and iconography in any language. The illustrations are unsatisfactory.

G. K. Loukomski. *L'Architecture Religieuse Russe du XIᵉ siècle au XVIIᵉ siècle*. Leroux, Paris, 1929. A vast and sumptuous volume consisting mainly of plates in collotype. The collection is, however, incomplete and unrepresentative.

In English

Rosa Newmarch. *The Russian Arts*. London, 1916. Two sparsely illustrated chapters deal briefly with the subject of architecture.

The *Encyclopaedia Britannica* (14th edition only) contains a short article.

TRANSCAUCASIA, ETC.
Armenia and Georgia

H. F. B. Lynch. *Armenia*. 2 vols. London, 1901. A travel book of the first order. Contains much good descriptive matter on Armenian architecture, and numerous illustrations, especially of Ani.

G. T. Rivoira. *Moslem Architecture, its Origins and Development*. Oxford, 1918. (Originally published at Milan in 1914.) Contains a considerable section on Armenia, not badly illustrated.

Josef Strzygowski. *Die Baukunst der Armenier und Europa*. Vienna, 1918. An immense and exhaustive work in two volumes, dealing also with the extension of Armenian influence westwards.

Johannes Schweiger. *Armenische Kunst, Elemente des Baues und Schmückens vor und nach dem Jahre 1000*.

Walter Bachmann. *Kirchen und Moscheen in Armenien und Kurdistan*. Leipzig, 1913. Contains an excellent set of collotype plates, mainly of churches in the Lake Van region (Southern Armenia, now Turkey).

Georg Tschubinaschwili (Chubinashvili). *Untersuchungen zur Geschichte der Georgischen Baukunst*. I. Band. Die Kirchen des Dschuari-Typs. Filser, Augsburg. Publication delayed indefinitely.

Jurgis Baltrušaitis. *Études sur l'Art Médiéval en Géorgie et en Arménie*. Leroux, Paris, 1929. A large, costly, and delightful book, in which a careful analysis is made of the systems of ornament in use in Transcaucasia. The hundred splendid plates in collotype depict details, but do not show buildings as a whole.

Rumania

G. Balş. *Influences Arméniennes et Géorgiennes sur l'Architecture Roumaine.* Communication faite au IIIe Congrès des Études Byzantines (Athènes, 1930). Imprimerie 'Datina Românească', Vălenii-de-Munte, 1931. Short letterpress and a considerable number of instructive pictures of Rumanian and Transcaucasian churches.

General works

Josef Strzygowski. *Origin of Christian Church Art.* Oxford, 1923. Contains many scattered references to Armenia. Among the same author's numerous works in German, the most convenient for a short summary of his theories is *Die Bildende Kunst des Ostens*, Leipzig, 1916. It is not easy to understand this author's important works, whether in the original or in translation.

O. M. Dalton. *East Christian Art.* Oxford, 1925. A fine volume, published at an extravagant price. It follows the plan of the same writer's *Byzantine Art and Archaeology*, and British Museum *Guide to Early Christian and Byzantine Antiquities*, but with the addition of a section on architecture. Various other writers' views on Armenia are summarised here.

Charles Diehl. *Manuel d'Art Byzantin.* Auguste Picard, Paris. New edition in two volumes, 1925–6. The only book giving a detailed and comprehensive review of the entire subject in lucid language. Affords excellent *résumés* of the various problems connected with Armenian architecture.

INDEX

When *def.* follows an entry, some explanation of the word will be found on the page referred to. Numbers in italics refer to text-figures: those in heavy type to plates

Printed in U.S.A. by
NOBLE OFFSET PRINTERS, INC.
NEW YORK, N.Y. 10003